Odd(ly) Enough

Praise for *Odd(ly) Enough*

"In a fast-paced world where it's easy to feel lost, this was a refreshing and humorous reminder to stay focused on my purpose. Her heartwarming and silly personal stories combined with passionate words of encouragement got me feeling like I'm ready to conquer the world!"

—Tiffany Jenkins, author and vlogger
of Juggling the Jenkins

"I loved *Odd(ly) Enough* from page one. It's a beautiful reminder of how God has a great and unique purpose for each one of us."

—Susannah Lewis (Whoa Susannah) author,
podcaster, and humorist

"For everyone who's been held prisoner by the box the world has put you in, felt compelled to hang drapes on the walls and move the furniture in, *Odd(ly) Enough* reminds us to bust out, break free, and believe that we are—and have always been—enough."

—Melissa Radke, author of *Eat Cake, Be Brave*

"My reaction to the first few words of *Odd(ly) Enough* was, *I need to hang out with this woman!* Her humor, her transparency (my favorite way to relate), her stories—I loved it all. But it was her hard-won wisdom and humble willingness to lay it all bare before our sweet Jesus that kept me turning the pages. Don't miss this one, y'all! I may reread it, slower this time!"

—Shellie Rushing Tomlinson, speaker, radio host, and author of *Devotions for the Hungry Heart*

"Her story is proof I was never alone. The truth that is laid out in this book is something I wish I would have read, known, and understood years ago."

—Courtney Grill, Mrs. Alabama 2017

"*Odd(ly) Enough* is a meeting place for the broken, the hurt, and the lost. Jesus will meet you in the pages of this book where He will undoubtably bring healing and restoration. Thank you, Carolanne, for your vulnerability and obedience in fulfilling your calling. This book is life."

—Hannah Martin, Owner of Ruby's Rubbish

Odd(ly) Enough

Enough

STANDING OUT
WHEN THE
WORLD BEGS YOU
TO FIT IN

CAROLANNE MILJAVAC

SHILOH RUN  PRESS

An Imprint of Barbour Publishing, Inc.

© 2018 by Carolanne Miljavac

Print ISBN 978-1-68322-789-2

eBook Editions:
Adobe Digital Edition (.epub) 978-1-68322-960-5
Kindle and MobiPocket Edition (.prc) 978-1-68322-963-6

Published by Shiloh Run Press, an imprint of Barbour Publishing, Inc., 1810 Barbour Drive, Uhrichsville, Ohio 44683, www.shilohrunpress.com

Our mission is to inspire the world with the life-changing message of the Bible.

Member of the
Evangelical Christian
Publishers Association

Printed in the United States of America.

In loving memory of
Ansley Abigail Smith

Contents

INTRODUCTION

*"My grace is sufficient for you,
for my power is made perfect in weakness."*
2 CORINTHIANS 12:9

Isn't it odd how God works? All the mysterious ways His plans come together with who He crafted us to be.

Have you ever taken the time to look back on all the moments you didn't think you'd survive, and recognized the purpose in your pain? Or maybe you've been stuck in the mud, unable to see any value in your struggle. Sometimes we get so bogged down by self-doubt that we can't see any potential for a better life. But know this: the greatest lie the enemy has ever whispered into your thoughts is that you aren't *enough*.

Have you ever had thoughts like this scamper through your mind?

You're not...

Good enough.

Smart enough.

Pretty enough.

Rich enough.

Kind enough.

Talented enough.

Loved enough.

Enough already, Satan! We get it! The evil one, the fallen angel determined to destroy those carrying the Spirit of Christ, is on a mission to convince us of all the things we know to be true about *him*. He hates the potential and redemption of those more powerful than he'll ever be. The misfits. The oddballs. The unqualified. The ones called to defy the standards of the world and stand in his way.

Yes, we are easy targets. We emerge from ditches, broken hearts, and bondage. Minds can be easily manipulated when spirits are broken. This was true for me. I wanted nothing more than to fit in from the time I was a child. By society's standards, I was poor white trash from a trailer park. Destined to become a teen mom and a drug addict, contributing nothing to society and living out my days in poverty. Many times I attempted to prove society right. Believe me when I tell you I tried really hard to throw my life away. Every inkling of purpose that crept up in my heart was immediately shoved down in disbelief. I know you've been there too. I didn't know it then, but God had other plans. What I was blind to back then, I now can see clearly. This is exactly how it needed to be: I needed to make mistakes so I could look back and marvel at the miracle of God's plan for my life.

It took a lot of wandering in the wilderness to

build the character I'd need for His calling. I was weak in my wilderness, and like 2 Corinthians 12:9 says, it is there that *His* power is made perfect. It is in our greatest moments of imperfection, when we are broken and humbled, aware of our need for God, that He comes in and shows us the beauty in our ashes. So everything that we think makes us an outcast is actually what makes us. . .oddly. . .*enough*. If you've ever felt insignificant, out of place, uncomfortable, or unqualified, I want to encourage you that it doesn't matter where you come from, what you've done, or what has been done to you. You have been qualified by the character built in your fall. The hardest parts of your life have given you the greatest value.

By the time you finish this book, I trust you'll believe that with all of your heart. I'm going to be completely bare, vulnerable, and transparent with my own life stories. A little bit of good alongside a whole lot of bad and ugly. Through poverty, molestation, bullying, sex, drugs, depression, and tragedy, God never gave up on me, and He'll never give up on you. So let's get naked. Okay, not legiterally. Keep your clothes on. Just keep reading.

CHAPTER 1

Who Do You Think You Are?

See what great love the Father has lavished on us,
that we should be called children of God! And that
is what we are! The reason the world does not
know us is that it did not know him.
1 John 3:1

A young girl waits anxiously, her face flushed red with embarrassment as her mother swipes the card *again*. Groans and eye rolls from the other shoppers in line weigh heavy on her shoulders. Determined to leave with *something* for her family to eat that night, her mother continues removing items from the buggy and swiping the card—yet again. As they walk away with nothing more than a pack of ramen noodles, the snickers behind them take root...a seed of insecurity planted itself deep inside the girl's spirit.

That young girl was me, and those snickers never

seemed to fade. The grocery store gamble was a frequent occurrence for us at the Walmarts. (If you're wondering when Walmart became plural, in the South it *always* was.) I was born and raised southern through and through—a girl from a small country town called Jasper, Alabama. Where sweet tea is the only option, "Yes, ma'am" means you were raised right, and everyone hugs hello and goodbye. If you've ever seen *Varsity Blues* or *Friday Night Lights*, it's pretty much what our town was like. Friday night high school football was life, everyone hung out at the mall, Mom dropped you and a friend off at the old, one-screen movie theater where teens in the back row made out while younger kids pointed and giggled. Summers were spent hopping hay bales, running barefoot on gravel roads, and riding bikes through the neighborhood hands-free. Being a country kid was so much fun.

When do we lose that carefree, life-loving spirit of a child? Maybe you can pinpoint your moment. Let me tell you about mine.

My mom and dad divorced when I was two years old. And I'm thankful they did. Dad would often go to the grocery store and return *three weeks later. . .* drunk and begging to stay. My dad can be quite the charmer. He's funny, lighthearted, kind, and a delight to be around. But he's also very selfish. He was a fantastic drummer, but his rock-and-roll dreams and drinking always took priority over his family. After my parents divorced, there is a pretty big chunk of time where he is missing from my memories. Dad was always in and out of our lives, and my mom was left to raise three young children by herself. She had several jobs at a time—cutting hair all day, working retail all night. Anything she could do just to keep our heads above water. And while she worked, my siblings and I spent a lot of time at our granny's house after school and on weekends.

I *loved* being at my granny's house. I didn't even care that she locked the screen door to keep us from running in and out because the air conditioner was running. "I'm not paying to cool down the whole neighborhood! In er out, in er out. Pick one. Just stay out there. *Murder, She Wrote* is comin' on. If you get thirsty, use the hose pap!" (Translation: water hose. I still say "hose pipe." It drives my Missouri-raised husband crazy.)

Granny lived in a nice middle-class neighborhood where you could hear the fountain splashing in the pond, birds chirping, ducks quacking, balls bouncing off bats at the park, and children giggling on the playground. An atmosphere ringing with sounds of a good life.

I loved the long and wide driveway we could ride

bikes on. I loved the basketball hoop where I spent hundreds of hours playing Around the World, dancing around dog turds to get the ball out of the grass. I loved the yard full of prickly stickers that would get stuck in your feet if you weren't careful. It seemed so *huge* for hide-and-seek. I loved the trampoline with missing springs that would pinch your skin if you happened to land on one while playing Popcorn.

The pond full of ducks was right across from Granny's house. She kept huge tin garbage cans by her house full of duck feed. I loved playing in the feed, scooping it out, and tossing it to the birds. A lost baby duck would often make its way over by her house, and my granny would take it in and raise it. *Ahhh.* I giggle just thinking about how many grown ducks would fly into Granny's yard with their nails painted in her favorite colors so we'd know the ducks were hers. When her adopted duck babies would drop into her backyard to say hi, she could call them by name. It was routine for Granny to strut her happy self right into the middle of the road in front of her house and stop traffic so the ducks could safely cross over. Her glare dared the drivers to even think about honking at her. Granny loved those ducks. I loved that place. It was so different from the run-down, roach-infested trailer park my family lived in.

My siblings and I would get so excited when our

cousins were around on holidays. We had more kids to play games with, and it was always a lot of fun. . . until one game of hide-and-seek ruined it for me.

I have two aunts. One always seemed a little wilder than the other. She had lots of tattoos, wore Daisy Dukes, smoked cigarettes, and had crazy-colored hair. She had three sons and a daughter. One of her sons was only a year older than me; at that time, I was around five and he was six. We often stuck together during hide-and-seek, basketball, bike riding, and tag. One day we were hiding behind my granny's bedroom door, standing side by side, and I felt him put his hand on my butt. It made me feel uncomfortable and weird, so I moved away and removed his hand, but I didn't want to make a big deal of it. We were so little, I didn't even understand why it made me feel uneasy.

I pretty much forgot about that incident until his advances grew even bolder. One day we were in my granny's bed watching a movie and resting while the adults prepared food and watched football or car races. My papa was all about watching some car racing with his eyes closed while he snored. It drove us nuts. (I wanna kick something when my husband does it. *You're asleep! Let me change the channel!*) No matter how careful we kids were, Papa always woke up the moment our little fingers touched the remote. So we would retreat to my granny's room to rest and watch something more our style. . .like *The Sandlot*. My cousin and I were watching Smalls learn what a s'more was when suddenly, my cousin lifted up the blanket and told me to look. He had pulled his pants down. I was caught so off guard. I have a little brother, so I knew that boys and girls are different, but I just knew it wasn't right for me to see his privates like that. He grabbed my hand and tried to get me to touch him. I jerked away and ran from the room. I remember looking around at all the adults talking, laughing, and watching TV and just feeling like I would cause a big problem if I told. I didn't want to get in trouble or get him in trouble if it wasn't a big deal. Plus, we always had so much fun with our cousins, and I didn't want to ruin that. I did my best to avoid him after that.

Unfortunately, that wasn't the end of it. The last time he touched me inappropriately, we were playing hide-and-seek, and I was hiding by myself. My head was under my granny's comforter, but my body was kind of hanging out. I felt someone begin to kiss my stomach, so I quickly pulled up the comforter and saw it was him. I was mortified, but that was nothing compared to the embarrassment I felt when I looked over and saw his mother's boyfriend staring at us. He had walked in and saw what was happening. But he just stood there. Staring. He never said a word. I felt my blood get hot and my face get red. I wanted to cry *and* disappear. I tossed the comforter back over my head trying to hide from the situation, hoping everyone would just go away. After a few minutes, I mustered up the courage to crawl out from under the comforter. Nobody was there. I was so nervous walking down the hall toward the rest of my family. I had no idea what everyone knew or what they would say. I wasn't sure if I was in trouble. All I knew was that I was so embarrassed. I didn't want anyone to even look at me.

But when I walked out, not a word was said; nobody even glanced at me funny. The kids had all gone outside to play, the women were talking in the kitchen, and the men were watching TV. This meant one of two things to me. Either he told them, and nobody cared because it wasn't a big deal; or he didn't tell them because it wasn't a big deal. Either way, I felt like I was the only one feeling something was wrong. So, in my mind, I was the weirdo. From this point I kept the incidents to myself and kept my distance from my cousin. I pretended nothing had happened. But a few years later, I found myself in a similar situation yet again.

My oldest cousin, whom I'll call Jenny, was the cool, pretty, older cousin, and everyone just seemed to love her. My older sister usually hung out with

Jenny at the family get-togethers. They were way too cool for our kid games. I didn't know much about her, but I knew that she sometimes lived with my granny. From what I gathered while eavesdropping on conversations (I was a secret spy, and really good at it), she was always running away from home. My granny and papa loved Jenny so much that they always let her stay with them to keep her from hitchhiking with strangers or running off with some boy. There were a couple of times the police had to find her and bring her home. As a child, I didn't think a whole lot about these things. Jenny just seemed wild like my aunt.

One day I was at my granny's house, and Jenny was living there at the time. I'm not sure where my brother and sister were. But she asked if I wanted to play a game with her. In her *room*. *What?!* The coolest room ever that I was *never* allowed in. I was so excited. I had always wanted to snoop around in there. Also, I couldn't believe my cool cousin wanted to hang out with me. She told me she wanted to play pretend. Like house. We would be husband and wife, and she would tell me and show me about some husband and wife things I didn't know about. She put me on the bed and kissed me. I didn't like it, but I didn't want her to get mad at me either. She put her tongue in my mouth, and my mind just shut down. I went to another place. I took myself away from the complete discomfort of rolling on the bed with her. I had no idea how to process what she was doing. I remember having my arms locked in close to my body because I didn't want to put them around her. When she was done making out with me, I didn't cry. I didn't feel sad. I felt overwhelmingly embarrassed and confused. I felt unsafe. I was so bewildered and annoyed that this stuff kept happening to me. Did it seem like I *wanted* to do these things? Was I supposed to? Why did I feel so gross? I was about seven years old at the time and still harbored what happened with my other cousin. I felt the same confusion—*If this is normal, then why do I feel so ashamed? If this is shameful, then why are they doing it?* But the biggest question was, *Why me?*

Some time later, I was at home watching TV when someone came to our door. I don't remember who it was, but this person told my mom that Jenny had been shot and killed. I think she was about fifteen and was dating a man in his thirties. He picked her up from middle school one day, and they were in his car. For some reason he shot her, then waited too long to call an ambulance, and she died on his floorboard.

When my mom told us Jenny had been killed, everyone started sobbing. I felt like I needed to get out of our living room. So I ran outside to our little red swing set. I didn't rush out there to cry, though. Instead, I felt a brief wave of relief. I wouldn't have to worry about being near her anymore. I wouldn't have to "play house" or feel weird and ashamed every time I saw her at family get-togethers. These emotions were immediately followed by guilt. Then a wave of sadness, because I hadn't wanted her to die. Next came feeling confused and overwhelmed. This was too heavy a burden for a child to carry. Too many mixed emotions for a nine-year-old to feel.

And guess who was right there, waiting to drop some pretty heavy strongholds into my thoughts? . . . The enemy.

This was a perfect setup for him. I was too young to understand my feelings. I didn't know enough about God or the enemy to know that what happened wasn't my fault. I didn't know that my self-destructive thoughts weren't really me. And so began the identity crisis. The false I Am's. I Am. . .

Weird.

Dirty.

Different.

Weak.

Bad.

Wrong.

Unsafe.

Hopeless.

Guilty.

Ashamed.

By nine years old. *Nine. This* is how I saw myself. I identified with the bad things that had happened to me and the wrong feelings I had about them. I was a victim. I was trash. I was wrong.

I should have told someone. *Why didn't you tell anyone? Did you like it? No. No! Then why didn't you say something? It's your fault. You can't tell anyone now, because she died. You can't ruin her memory like that. Everyone will hate you for waiting until now. Just keep it to yourself.*

The roots grow deeper.

Your secrets make you sick.

The truth? I'm freaking out a little as I share this with the world. But I know someone reading my story can relate. Perhaps it's you. And I need you to know you're not alone. It's not your fault, you're not weird, and your bad experience doesn't define you. But it will heavily influence how you feel about yourself if you keep it in the shadows and refuse to deal.

One of the things the enemy wants to steal away from you is knowledge of *who* you really are. Your life is what he hopes to deprive you of. He doesn't want you to experience the amazing life God has planned for you. He knows he has already lost the fight for your soul, so he will do everything he can to manipulate your thoughts. And the way you think about yourself has everything to do with the way you live your life.

Y'all, so many of us navigate through life with a complete misunderstanding of who we really are. Know this: Your identity can't be found in the minds and mouths of others. You are not defined by the number in your bank account, the brand of clothing on your back, the house you live in, the mistakes you've made, what's been done to you, or what you've done to others. Your value as a human being is not determined by your social status. Your potential is not limited by the opinions of others. You are *not* dirty, gross, or to blame for the sins of others.

Your *purpose* will be achieved as you allow every lesson you've learned through your hardships to mold your character for the better. You can turn every harsh word into a loving sentence toward someone who needs it—just as you once did. You can take every side-eye and twist it into a smile for a stranger who seems down. You can shape every struggle you've faced into a story that the wounded heart needs to hear.

———

In the coffee aisle, a mama with her hands full tried her best to push the huge, car-shaped buggy out of my way. On this rare occasion, I was shopping all alone, and I felt an immediate connection, for I know the struggle of shopping with kids all too well. Her toddler was passed out, drooling on her chest in one of those wrap baby holders, and her son sat in the front of the cart. She smiled and complimented my shoes. I thought how sweet she was to show kindness to me while her hands were so full.

As I continued to browse, a whisper I've come to know well slid into my thoughts: "Offer to help push the buggy to her car." Of course, I felt uncomfortable at the thought of approaching her. What would she think? *Will she get defensive? Will I seem self-righteous?* I passed her in the checkout as I was heading to my car, and I hurried up so I could get my stuff put away and then go back in the store.

She was in the checkout and was also on the phone. She looked anxious. I didn't want her to see me staring, so I walked past and tried to hear what she was saying. (Imagine me in the background, pacing back and forth trying not to look like a creeper while pumping myself up to step in.) I overheard that there was a problem with her account, and she was asking her husband to come and pay for their groceries. As soon as I heard her words and saw the shoppers in line growing annoyed, my thoughts immediately flashed back to how I felt as a little girl when my mom's card wouldn't go through. I didn't hesitate for one second. It became so clear why God had nudged me to go back in the store.

I walked up quietly, put my hand on her shoulder, and said, "Can I please take care of this for you?" She stared at me like a deer in the headlights. I told her I knew they had the money, but that I had come back in to help her with her cart because I wanted to do something nice for a fellow mama, and this was just an extra opportunity for her to bless me by letting me help out.

I could feel the eyes of other shoppers staring a hole right through me as I swiped my card. I looked back at them, then looked at the cashier and chirped loudly, "My bank holds my account all the time without warning me. And I always find out in a backed-up, frustrated grocery line. Makes you wanna shout to everyone, I *have* the money!" Some chuckled, while others may have been annoyed and judgmental. But just *maybe* someone felt a stirring in their own spirit to help next time. I don't know. But I do know that's how God works. I don't know what it meant to her, but God did. It wasn't about me.

I'm not some outstanding person. I simply made a choice to walk back in when it would've been easier to load up and head home. But God knew a piece of me would be touched in that moment. The piece of my heart that broke for my own mom gave me the compassion to step in. God helped me take my twenty-seven-year-old memory of shame and use it for good—by paying it forward. He used a part of my past that made me feel different and "less than" to show me I'm odd(ly) enough.

You can ask God to mold something good from the struggles you've gone through. You do have a choice. You can take your dust and trade it for diamonds...to be the shiny spot in a world desperate for sparkle. Or...you can hold on to your darkness, let it take root in your heart, and live a life of mediocrity. I don't wanna wander in the wilderness when God has a better way. *Be still. Listen.* He'll bring opportunities for you to do something good for someone. And trust me when I tell you it'll heal your heart every time you follow through.

Had anyone given me words of encouragement like this up until about three years ago, I would have rolled my eyes hard enough to see my brain. I immediately would have come to my own defense: "It's real easy for someone to say that when they haven't lived my awful life. How dare you tell me to make the most out of hardships you know nothing of! There's no good to be found in poverty, an alcoholic absent dad, innocence interrupted by molestation, bullying, suicidal thoughts, cancer, and loss. The Bible may say that God works for the good in *all* things, but I can't accept there is good to come from any of this."

Victim Mentality

"Victim" was a part of my identity. If I wasn't a victim, then I was what. . .to blame? I didn't accept that. So I clung to *victim*. It was all I knew. It came easy to me, and it gave me a great excuse to act out. Why would I ever stretch myself to be better if I'd always be a victim? I was unworthy of joy because joy had always been stolen from me. These thoughts become excuses for bad behavior—the result of never dealing with something that has hurt us.

The problem with a victim mentality is that whatever you think to be true about your life is followed by actions toward that end. In other words, if you expect to be a victim, then you'll look for ways to be victimized. I put myself in so many bad positions when I was a teenager. I already viewed myself as damaged, so I was continually placing myself in situations that could hurt me even further. I hung out with the wrong crowd doing things I knew I shouldn't do. I went to raves overflowing with ecstasy and glowsticks—I was that girl dancing circles in a techno trance, covered in sweat and smoking cigarettes. Looking back, I am completely shocked I never required emergency treatment for an overdose. I seriously just didn't care. I tried almost every drug you can think of. It's hard to believe that I never went to jail, got raped, or got myself killed. In a way, I can't help but think I almost wanted to—I mean, I tried to throw my life away over and over again. Completely reckless. I'd take any pill I was handed. Drink whatever. I even smoked crystal meth out of tinfoil once. Lit the fire until the white smoke rose and inhaled it deep into my lungs. I wanted to be the girl who was down for anything. The life of the party, while dying inside. Why not? Everyone thought my family was white trash anyway, and that was what was always expected of me. The girl from the trailer park. It's *who I am*, right? I shudder when I think about it, but I now understand why I was so self-destructive.

When you stuff shame into your baggage, it's hard to zip it shut. You can sit on it, jump on it, put all your weight on it. . .but it's always there, never really closed off. And just when you think you've convinced yourself it didn't really happen to you, it comes back like a lucid nightmare. All too real. It will haunt the back of your thoughts and manifest itself in your decisions. It takes root in your heart and your mind, always lingering over you. The harder you try to pretend it isn't there, the more miserable it makes you.

Think about it. If I feel dirty and gross, will I have

self-esteem? Will I be capable of self-love? If I don't love myself, will I take care of myself? If I don't feel worthy of love, will I have healthy relationships?

No. I will go out and get what I believe I deserve. I will live a life reflective of my decisions—decisions based on the lies behind my identity crisis.

Girl, you gotta reach down deep and pull out that shame by the roots. It hurts, and it's scary. But it's completely necessary.

But *how*? How do I let this go? you ask. Start by discovering who God says you are. Read of His love for you. If you don't know who you really are, you won't be able to live in the now and let go of the past. If you identify with what's been done to you and continue gripping it tight, how can you ever move forward? You can't heal something you won't deal with. You can't deal with something you refuse to acknowledge.

I want to encourage you to bring your wound to the surface. Feel it. Talk about it. You can do that in therapy, with a friend, in prayer, or through journaling. Let yourself cry, curse, and hurt. I promise the pain will fade and you'll be able to move forward. We stuff hard things down to try to avoid the feelings that come with them. The experiences with my cousins left me feeling ashamed, guilty, dirty, anxious, and gross. I didn't like those feelings at all, so instead of talking to someone about it, I tried to convince myself it never happened. But it was *always* there. My buried secret. And it was making me sick. I needed to get it out in the open! It took me thirty years to let it go, because it wasn't until then that I realized who I was in Christ. I will share how that happened later on, but one of the first things revealed to me after I wholeheartedly gave up my life was that I needed to lay down my pain. I needed to let go of control. I needed to step away from my feelings and trust God to deal in *His way* with those who hurt me. I realized it wasn't my burden to bear.

I think what makes it hard for us to let go is feeling like we're admitting it was okay. But that's a lie of the enemy. Allow yourself to feel the pain, the hurt, the shame, whatever it is your experience bubbles up to the surface. Cry your heart out. Cry so hard you throw up if you need to. At some point the pain will run out and the tears will stop flowing. And when that moment comes, lift up your head, take a deep breath, wipe your face, and say out loud, "This is no longer my burden, Lord. I give it to You." That is "laying it down." Bring it to the surface, feel it, let it out, lay it down, and walk away. Deal so you can heal.

And once you walk away, *never* go back. Trust God to be the One to take the wrongs and make them right. It's not your job. You are made new as a child of God. That means the things before today no longer exist. You can be a new person, pursuing a new life. No longer held back by the past. No longer wandering around in the wildernes—lost, hurting, and confused. No longer using what you've been through to sabotage your life!

Ready for some hard-to-hear truths? Sometimes we don't want to let things go because they have become our reasons for why we are the way we are. Why we do the things we do. They are our excuses for bad behavior. *How can anyone be mad at me when I've been through the things I have?*

Not My Fault

It's not my fault I have a drinking problem.

It's not my fault I have trust issues and sabotage all my relationships.

It's not my fault I stopped caring about myself.

It's not my fault I am unhealthy.

I have worked with countless women as a health/fitness/life coach, and something almost everyone has in common when they aren't where they want to be is a lack of responsibility for where they are. When I ask, "How did you get to a place where you're unhappy and unhealthy?" I almost never get the response, "I've been making poor choices."

The reply typically involves the word *because*:

Because I am going through a divorce.

Because I lost a loved one.

Because I was abused.

I drink too much *because* my dad left when we were little.

I binge eat *because* we unexpectedly lost my mom back in April.

I don't take care of myself *because* my boyfriend emotionally abused me for two years.

Not only are you identifying with what's been done to you, but you're using it as an excuse to self-destruct. Sometimes we use it as an excuse to do things that feel good *now* but hurt us *later*.

I want to make something crystal clear: *it is not your fault* when someone or something hurts you.

However, the way you react is *all you*. Should you choose to react negatively, your decisions could actually become what someone else is trying to overcome. You have been impacted by the decisions of others, so make sure the mark you make doesn't become someone else's excuse to self-destruct. Break the cycle.

Will Smith recently had a Facebook video saying this exact thing about fault and responsibility. "You don't have to accept blame for things that were out of your control, but you do have to take responsibility for how you react." Decisions you make in response to something are *your* decisions.

Let's say you deal with a death in the family by binge eating junk food and gaining twenty pounds—which results in you feeling sick, tired, and unhappy. You aren't sick, tired, and unhappy because a loved one passed away. You are sick and unhealthy because you *chose* to respond by putting an excess of harmful food into your body. Ohhh, have I ever been there.

It feels kind of good to feel bad sometimes. It tastes good. . .chowing down on cake and Funyuns (my go-to) with no care for how it's affecting your body. It feels good to drink away your pain and pretend to be having fun. It might bring your flesh momentary satisfaction to sleep with someone and feel something other than lonely and unwanted. But then you're left with a stomachache, a hangover, a dirty regret, and no solution to your problems.

Let's say you carry around the painful memory of abuse like me. You decide to chase away that pain with alcohol instead of dealing with it (like I did many times). You get drunk, get behind the wheel, and sideswipe a vehicle on the interstate, causing several accidents and the injury of five people. Is it your abuser who drove drunk and caused the wreck? No. That was *your* decision. Your choices are your responsibility, and now your choices have caused harm to others. What if your abuser was abused? He or she grew up beaten by an alcoholic dad, and instead of dealing and healing started making bad choices just like you did. Now *they* drink to handle the pain, and their drunken rage overflows onto you. Somebody at some point has to make the decision to do what is best for themselves and others. Somebody has to break the cycle. I know it's hard, and that's why the words that take up space in your mind matter.

Some of us claim we have no idea how to let go when the truth is, we just don't want to. You identify as a victim and therefore have no idea how to live without pain. You know discovering who you truly are will mean letting go of living in your self-destructive pattern. If you're being honest, you might be ashamed to admit you aren't ready to let go of momentary satisfactions of the flesh.

Let's be *brutally* honest here: bad decisions are easy. Living the life you claim you so desperately want will require effort and sacrifice. Sometimes doing the right thing or making the changes in your life necessary for your joy and purpose will cost you friendships with people who don't understand or who feel threatened by the changes you're making. Having the healthy habits you need for your mind, body, and soul will mean sacrificing some bad ones that you've become reliant on. That's what makes living for God and truly loving yourself difficult. You can't do all the things that taste good and feel good right now because you're deciding it's not worth the cost and consequences you're paying later. Are you avoiding dealing and healing because you don't want to admit that a better life is within your grasp, and you just aren't willing to reach?

Please reach.

But don't just reach. Claw, scratch, grasp, and tumble toward change. It's worth every ounce of effort. The feeling of joy fills the void so much better than food or booze. You have a light in you. Yes, *you*! You have so much to give if you choose to live. I want you to make a decision today to step away from your past. I want you to know without a shadow of a doubt that you are *so much more* than the number in your bank account, the brand of clothing on your back, the names that one guy called you in eighth grade, or even your biggest mistakes. You are *not* defined by what has been done to you or what you have done. Your identity isn't revealed in the minds and mouths of those around you.

Deep down into your soul, God whispers the character He created in you. He leaves hints of your gifts, draws a path to your passion. You don't have to listen to the world. You are His greatest creation. All of your suffering, grief, regret, guilt, and shame can make you new when mixed with love. So next time the enemy asks you who you think you are, let him know. Let him know through your refusal to settle for anything less than everything God created you to be. Oddly enough, everything He created you to be comes together as a result of the hell the enemy puts you through.

What the devil doesn't know is that when he puts you through hell, you take fuel from the fire!

Ohhh daaang. Did y'all just get excited? Am I the only one waving my hands like "Sister, you better preach it!" Y'all better get on my level right now. That spirit of yours is aching to rejoice. Give in. You're free to celebrate the bright future you have ahead of you in your newfound God-fidence. Be set free!

Let 'em get set free, God, I pray. Amen.

CHAPTER 2

Don't Look at Me

God is within her, she will not fall;
God will help her at break of day.
Psalm 46:5

When I was eight years old, I was at a friend's pool party. I needed to borrow a swimsuit, so while everyone was out back I walked around their house coveting like crazy. Wishing I lived like this family did. I would pretend it was my house and that I had all the things they had. Two parents, nice clothes, a pool, tons of Hamburger Helper in the kitchen cabinets, my own room with a see-through phone that glowed in neon colors when my boyfriend Zack Morris called.

I was really, really good at pretending to be someone else. Someone who wasn't weird, poor, ashamed, and insecure. So that day I decided, *I'm gonna swim like them too.* I hadn't even learned to swim yet, but that didn't stop me from walking right off the diving board as though I knew exactly what I was doing. I didn't even hesitate to jump. The water swallowed me whole. I kicked and flailed my arms around in the exact opposite way a person swims and. . .shocker, I went nowhere. Instead, I sank right to the bottom. I watched the light reflect off the water as my toes scraped the floor of the pool. I kid you not, one of my first thoughts was *I should gather up all these pool rings while I'm down here. . . .* I know, oddball. But reality set in right after, and I went into "I imme-diately regret this decision" mode. As panic started to well up, my friend's dad came barreling toward me. He swooped me up and pulled me to safety. I scared them to death. They kept asking me why I had jumped in the deep end if I couldn't swim. I had no response. No reason other than *I just did.* I was so embarrassed. But I did have a tendency to act first and think later. Then I thought, *They must really think I'm weird. . . . I am so weird.*

I was carrying some pretty heavy emotional chains at that time. The bricks in my backpack were marked with poverty, sexual abuse, and insecurity. Looking back, I can see that at such a young age I carried those chains right into the deep end of the pool and they hauled me straight to the bottom. I made a de-cision that could have gotten me killed—just to do it.

I also had a serious feeling that I could do whatever I believed I could do. I just missed the "crawl before you walk" part.

When I say I truly believed I could do anything, I mean legiterally anything. I decided I could do gymnastics one day. No training or anything, just watching the girls on TV do it. I thought, *She makes it look easy enough.* I could picture myself in my mind doing a flip and landing solid on my feet—no little hops—and pointing my fancy fingers up for a perfect score. So I got off my papa's recliner, walked over in front of the TV, and attempted a front flip. You know how when you're little and someone gets off a seesaw without telling you first, and it slams your behind down into the ground so hard you feel it ringing in your ears? That's how hard my forehead smacked my granny's living room carpet. I dang near knocked myself out cold. I stood up a little dazed and confused, thinking, *I didn't get any air on that and I can't understand why.* Ahhh, I'm laughing so hard right now replaying this in my mind. It hurt so *bad*, y'all. My forehead had the biggest egg right in the middle of it. I barely even jumped, and my arms stayed at my sides. Basically I just stood up and threw my face into the floor.

Granny ran in like, "What happened?"

I said, "I thought I could do a front flip."

Looking unamused, she said, "Why in the world

would you do that? You can't just do flips without any practice. Sit down. I'll go get the ice pack."

Murmuring under her breath in the sweetest southern accent as she walked off, "Just threw her face to the floor. Child ain't gotta licka sense."

Ohhh my. I hope y'all can picture how this played out in your head, because it was absolutely hilarious. Bless my granny's heart. I drove her nuts, but that's okay because with three daughters of my own now I am most definitely "payin' for my raisin'." (That's something southern grandmamas love to say while taking pleasure in all the payback their grandkids are serving up.)

But here's the thing. Impulsive is who I am. And although it's a characteristic that gets me in trouble at times, God knew it would also be the piece of me that would help me do what He called me for— so long as I wouldn't let my own thoughts keep me from fulfilling my potential.

But, unfortunately, those did get in the way. And y'all know why. A part of me felt like I couldn't escape being "less than" everyone else. I had a dirty secret, and it messed with my head for a very long time. I carried a bit of a chip on my shoulder and built a wall over the years to keep people from knowing me on a deeper level. If they got too deep, they might discover my secret. So I preferred to let my true self sink while they hung out with the girl on the surface. Oh dang, that was deep. (You may wanna reread it just to be sure you made the connection between the previous story and what I just said. Go on, I'll wait. . . .)

Have you ever held back who you *really* are for fear that people might see you as the monster you keep in the closet? That what's been done to you is who you are? That what you've done is who you are? And if they saw it, there'd be no going back. Your image and potential would be ruined.

From what I had heard preached in church, God already knew my secrets. . .which I found extremely mortifying. So what did I do? I ignored Him. I did what those of us who grow up in poverty do well: I kept moving forward. Stayed strong. Was totally fine. *I'm fine. I'm always fine.* Stayed on the defense. Always expecting others to look down on me.

In many ways, my humor was a tool so I could deflect reality. I would make a fool of myself to make people laugh or get people to like me. I knew the only reason the cool kids let me hang out with them was because I was so goofy. I did whatever they wanted me to. One day we were all standing out in front of the school waiting for our parents to pick us up. They said, "Hey, Carol, it would be so funny if you ran across the lawn and tripped in front of everyone." So I took off. In front of the entire school I slid across the lawn on my belly, as if it was an accident, just to make everyone laugh. It hurt and it was embarrassing, but I laughed it off like "Look at me: I'm the class clown." It's odd, but when I was the center of attention making people laugh, they were blind to the pain I was carrying. I was an extroverted introvert. I felt a strong call to entertain, and I badly wanted attention and recognition. But at the same time, I'd limit myself and hold myself back because I feared if they saw the real me it would confirm, yet again, that I wasn't enough.

Your purpose isn't meant to be used as a defense mechanism. No. It's supposed to set you free. Humor was always going to be a huge part of the calling on my life. But for a while, it wasn't setting me free; instead, it was helping me mask the pain I was experiencing. Being truly seen is so scary but absolutely necessary if you want to experience true joy. If you can love and embrace who God created you to be, you'll find the links to several of your broken chains. Knowing who He crafted you to be—*and why*—allows you to embrace your gifts and see them bloom into something you never knew existed. It truly removes the limits from what you can do.

What would you do if you fully trusted who you are? If you only knew what's waiting behind the doors God will open for you (when you're ready, of course)? Yes, walking through them means risk, vulnerability, and exposure. But what would you do if you truly trusted God to get you through each new experience? What does that look like for you? Think about it. . .write it. Then read it and pray over it every day. Over time you'll find yourself making little steps toward God's plan for you instead of ignoring it.

Please hear me. Beneath the surface, you—yes, you!—have a strong, capable, courageous spirit. And your realization of that truth is the enemy's worst nightmare. So he does his best to drown it out with others' opinions, distractions, to-do lists, comparison, guilt, shame, insecurity, and lies. It's your easily persuaded flesh that gets in the way. When I say "flesh," I mean mind and body separate from your soul. Your soul is who you really and truly are. Your emotions are manipulated by the world. Easily tampered with. Your feelings are heavily influenced by your surroundings. Your thoughts are messed with by the words of others. And if you allow yourself to feel a certain way depending on the actions and words of others, who are also heavily influenced by their surroundings, you'll always be an unstable mess. And this is where the enemy gets you. He plays with your emotions. He messes with your thoughts. He studies you. He knows you well. He will manipulate others to speak the exact words he has already planted in your thoughts—to confirm that you are untalented, unloved, hopeless, ugly, worthless. . .whatever you struggle with the most. He lies to you, and he uses other people to do it too. Let me ask you this: have you ever had someone come out of nowhere and completely discourage you right as you were about to make a positive change in your life?

But have you ever felt a conflict with those lies? That maybe you *are* capable and that's why you get your hopes up; that's why you feel afraid to fail? Because deep down your spirit remains, and it is a reflection of the truth. You know you *can*. You know you *could*. You know you're not who they say you are. Why do you keep seeing and dreaming visions of a better life, success, and purpose? *Because*, sister, that is the *truth*! How many bad decisions have you made—all stemming from a belief that you could do no better? How many times have you jumped in the deep end knowing you couldn't swim? I made countless wrong choices stemming from lies the enemy spoke to me.

I spiraled a bit in high school. Especially freshman year. The need I had to fit in and be accepted—along with the knowledge it would *never* happen—set me off on a series of careless, reckless, self-destructive choices. Y'all know that song about wishing you could be like the cool kids because they all seem to fit in? It could have been the theme song for my teenage years. I would do whatever the cool kids were doing. One night when I was a freshman in high school I was spending the night with my "friend." One of the pretty, popular girls. I was shocked I was even invited. She was having a small party, and I'm pretty sure no parents were there. We were drinking at first, and then some of the boys said they had some pills. I instantly had a knot in my stomach. I knew it was the wrong choice. I knew it was a bad idea. But this heavy, *heavy* chain of worthlessness pulled me under in that moment, and I swallowed what I was handed.

Are you letting your chains pull you under? What are you drowning in? Debt, alcohol, drugs, bad relationships, food, overwhelm, overload, doubt? These heavy burdens will take your life. We cry out in our own way. Sometimes we don't even realize we're doing it—pushing people away, being thoughtless with our safety, making rash decisions, destroying our health.

The last thing I remember from the party that night is being in a car with an older boy driving and one of the boys from my class in the backseat. I don't know what we were doing or where we were going. The boys were talking about the girls at school. The boy in the back (whom I kind of considered a friend) said, "I'm sorry, Carol, but I just don't think you are very pretty. You kind of look like a rat." He sat in the back laughing at his brutal honesty as if it was no big deal and he was such a good friend to tell me the truth. I was humiliated. Here I was feeling kind of cool to be hanging out with two of the popular boys, thinking they'd accepted me as a friend, and he just annihilated my self-esteem. The boy driving felt kind of bad and said, "I don't think that. I think you could be really pretty if you tried." (Ugh. I just let out the longest sigh writing this, remembering how awful I felt.) I just wanted to go home, but I was so messed up I didn't wanna get in trouble. So I did what I always did when these friends of mine tore me down: I made a joke of it. I turned around and made the ugliest face possible and said, "Well, you have to admit, I'm the best-looking rat you've ever seen." They laughed so hard, and I pretended it was fine. Next thing I knew, I woke up in the older boy's bed. With no idea how I got there. No idea what happened between the car ride and my waking up. I was immediately scared to death, wondering what I might have done while I was incoherent. The boy wasn't in the bed with me; he told me he slept on the floor. I'll honestly never really know if that's entirely true. Let me be clear: we didn't have sex. I would've known because I was a virgin at the time, and I had no signs of anything like that happening. But I don't remember any details. They said we went to Walmart. I can't even imagine how I must have looked, roaming Walmart with zero awareness of what I was doing. I do know that the people who saw me that night were getting exactly what I felt they expected from me. White trash, barefoot in the Walmarts, bound to end up pregnant.

I knew better.

And deep down you know better. Looking back, I realize that knot in my stomach was the Holy Spirit trying to protect me. Trying to guide me. I sometimes wonder if God shudders at the crap we put ourselves through before we break down and realize that we are worth more than this. Because of free will He has to allow us to walk through the fire. You can't trade ashes for beauty if you've never been burned. You won't be willing to let them go until the lesson is learned.

I wrote the following poem inspired by the concept from Isaiah 61:3, "Beauty for Ashes." It's about letting God trade you something beautiful when you hand Him your pain. Everything I had tried to hide from God was used by Him to create character in me—just what was needed to fulfill my purpose.

Beauty for Ashes

Everybody's wounded.
Check Facebook, I'll prove it.
Angry faces, politics, and trolls.
What do we do about it?
Let's take a poll.
You slap on a band-aid.
Carry it around.
Never let it heal,
Only slow you down.
When self-hate becomes essential,
Mediocre is your potential.
Don't believe it.
The qualified are called by character
    built in the fall.
I learned to forgive from my molester.
Perseverance from oppressors.
And the value of life, from cancer.
The struggle is where the lessons are learned.
If you wanna transform, you gotta get burned.
Healing of the heart can be acquired.
You can't trade ash for beauty
    without a *fire*.

Matthew 11:28 says, "Come to me, all you who are weary and burdened, and I will give you rest." It doesn't say, "Come to me when you've got it all figured out," or "Come to me once you've earned your grace." It just says, "Come to me."

I know so many who struggle believing that God accepts them as they are. Please remember that the sacrifice He made for you wasn't because you are so spotless and perfect. If you believe that Jesus died for all the things marking up your clean slate, then you must know you are loved through anything and everything. Aren't you tired of pretending? Isn't it exhausting carrying all those bricks around in your back pocket? God's burden is light—no guilt, no shame. You don't have to earn His love. You can simply let Him in and hand over your burden. If you struggle with feelings of worthlessness, remember this: if the value of something is reflected by the price paid for it, *Jesus gave up His flesh and blood* because your life *matters*. Your soul is loved, and there's nothing this world or your flesh can do to change that.

I can say without a doubt that God loves me and He loves you. I have gotten drunk at the bar and then driven home, risking the lives of others on the road. I have been the wild girl during Panama City Beach Spring Break, flashing my boobs to boys for beads (I'm so sorry, Mama). I've been lost in the lights at the club, high on ecstasy and grabbing for cigarettes someone tossed onto the floor. I've cursed God. I have blamed Him for all my problems and actively rebelled against all the things the church perceives as Christian. I let a boy take my virginity in an abandoned shack after sneaking out of the house with my best friend. (*Bam.* That's one secret I have *never* revealed. Wow. . .I thought I'd take that one with me to the grave. But I'm letting it go, y'all. Just laying it out there to leave it behind.) The guilt, shame, regret, and disgust I once harbored toward myself nearly destroyed what was meant to be a fruitful life. My true calling was interrupted by bad decisions founded on lies the enemy spoke to me. I can't tell you how many times I've thought to myself, *I'm just not a good person.* Many times life felt just too hard for me to bear. I didn't know if I could make it. . .or if I even wanted to. I once even considered that taking my own life just might be worth it—just to escape this world.

If you can relate to my story, I want you to know a few things. I'm *not* a cookie-cutter Christian who has it all together. None of us are. We all have a past, and we've all had unique experiences. Some of us just straight up feel lost. . .and *we're exactly who God is seeking.* The broken. The poor. The battered and bruised. The abused and confused. The meek and weary. I don't fit the mold of those behind a pulpit professing their love for Jesus. I once was lost, y'all. *Lost.* Lost in the club. Lost in the drugs. Lost in lies and lust that left me feeling. . .bad. You know that feeling I'm talking about? Just bad. Wrong. Not once did I ever give my body to my boyfriend without feeling ashamed right after. I thought it was just me. *I'm bad. I'm wrong. I'm dirty. I'm so weird that this makes me feel so wrong when it seems like everyone else is doing it just fine.* Do you know why I had these thoughts? Because that wasn't who I was. My spirit struggled so hard to make sure I knew that. This was a feeling I now know is called conviction.

If you are lost right now, you need to know that God is after you. He is *for* you, sister.

Don't ever let someone carrying the title of "Christian" make you feel like you are worth less than they are. Human beings are flawed, and that includes all who have decided to follow Jesus. This is nothing new. Luke 19 tells of a rich man named Zacchaeus who was a tax collector. And he certainly wasn't popular with the people. When Jesus traveled through Jericho, Zacchaeus scrambled ahead and climbed up a sycamore tree to get a better look at Jesus. Zacchaeus *sought* Him. Jesus recognized this, looked up, and told him to come down for He would be going to Zacchaeus's house. This announcement didn't go over well with the people who followed Jesus. They were angry that Jesus was going to the home of a man who was a sinner. *A sinner*, y'all! As if they weren't sinners themselves. Zaccaheus humbled himself before Jesus and promised to give back anything he had taken *times four*. In that moment, Jesus granted Zaccheus salvation, for *he too* was a son of Abraham.

> *"For the Son of Man came to seek*
> *and to save the lost."* (Luke 19:10)

Jesus explained to the people that He was seeking those who are lost, using this example: the shepherd will leave his flock to seek out and find the wandering sheep. There is no person, and I mean *no* person, whom Jesus will turn away if they humble themselves and seek out salvation. The truth? . . . Sometimes we don't like that, do we? We don't like the idea that someone who does not deserve our forgiveness could receive favor from our Lord. But there is no required standard of living to be met to make a person worthy of redemption. No pew is too clean for the dirt on your booty; it is a resting place for the praying sinner. If Jesus hung on that cross for the people ripping the flesh from His back, spitting on Him, mocking Him, and laughing as they hammered nails into His body, then whether anybody likes it or not, He also died for you. You know what else? It is *scriptural* that when a lost soul receives Jesus, we are to celebrate and rejoice that our brother or sister has been found.

I don't care how much you dislike a person, or even if they continue saying or doing things you don't like. You always—as a disciple of Christ (which is what all Christians are supposed to be)—should pray for and encourage others. If you can't, then you need to ask God to fill this weakness of your flesh with His strength. It is our job to bring people to Christ. Period. End of story. Condescension, judgment, criticism, and insults disguised as opinions will never make someone want what you claim you have. That kind of behavior is not a reflection of Christ. Jesus spoke to people with love—even those who were looked down on by the religious leaders.

It is always *love* that results in a change of heart. Never forget that love is kind and patient. There is a big difference between offering loving guidance to someone you feel could use a good word and condemning someone in order to make yourself feel superior. None of us, not one, is without sin. All sins may not be the same, but all sins are forgiven when you give your life to Jesus and acknowledge His sacrifice.

But if we walk in the light, as he is in the light, we have fellowship with one another, and the blood of Jesus, his Son, purifies us from all sin. (1 John 1:7)

It's true: the lost are loved. The strongest of testimonies often come from those who have been through the trenches. If the light of Christ is going to spread through the darkest of places, we need Christians willing to leave their comfort zones. We need those who understand how it feels to be broken, abused, and hopeless. Those who don't hold themselves on a higher pedestal than everyone else. Every time I share my story, I feel a tingle of fear. I grew up with the idea that I wasn't good enough, clean enough, sparkly enough to speak about my love for Jesus. I worried that people would hold me to a standard that I couldn't possibly live up to. But it's not other people I need to concern myself with, for I can always count on God's grace and love for me, flaws and all. Your differences—your struggles—are what allow God to use you to reach others in unique ways.

God is calling you. Yes, *even you*. Don't forget that when someone is pointing out your flaws, it's to distract others from their own skeletons. If you're reading this and feeling a bit of conviction, that's okay! We've all been there. Especially in a season of life when we are struggling and feeling confused. When we are low, we have a natural tendency to wanna drag someone down right along with us. It makes us feel better. But please make it your mission to lift others up.

If you genuinely want to make someone's life better or help them to see that they are making bad decisions, the best thing you can do is be an example. Show genuine interest in their life. Learn what they are going through—and why—by asking questions and listening. Be open minded to their circumstances. Speak humbly. Let your tone show you know you aren't perfect either. It's God's place to judge the world, and it's our place to inspire change in others through love. Love. That was Jesus, and that is what He passed on to His disciples. And *that* is why He left His Spirit to guide us and fill us with that same joy and love.

You know when someone is coming from a place of love—it's obvious, isn't it? You can tell if their words come from a place of genuine good intention or condescension. Think about these questions: How many people have you loved into the light? How many people have you criticized away from Christ? I'm not saying "zip your lips," but I am saying "be helpful, not hurtful." I'm not telling you to sugarcoat things either. Just check your motivations: are you really trying to help, or are you being arrogant?

I grew up so defensive because of my circumstances. I hated feeling like I was less than everyone else. And for a long time, I felt like I might as well not even try because my innocence was gone. I didn't feel worthy of a life for God, even though I was surrounded by Christians. My family started attending church when I was eight years old. We were there Sunday morning, Sunday night, and Wednesday night. I knew the Bible stories. I knew the rules. But I never understood anything about relationship and acceptance. I thought I had to live a certain way to be loved. I didn't understand that I am loved *regardless*.

So many people—Christians included—walk around as just shells of who they are meant to be because of fear that who they are isn't good enough. We hide behind religion, rules, and faults of others. But don't forget God knows your heart *and* your secrets. He sees you and accepts you for who you are; and when you have given control over to Him, He will shape you into who He created you to be. So stop living like "Don't look at me." Instead, let Him set you free.

CHAPTER 3

Rock-Bottom Revelation: Falling Forward

The LORD is close to the brokenhearted
and saves those who are crushed in spirit.
PSALM 34:18

When I graduated from college, I decided to move in with my boyfriend (now husband) and take the entire summer off to relax, party, and reward myself for barely earning a bachelor's degree. I got a job waiting tables to earn just enough for bills, food, cigarettes, and weekend fun. Truthfully, I was just procrastinating responsibility. Adulthood scared the crap out of me. Deep down, I was still resisting a belief that there wasn't much of a future for me. So I avoided adulthood by behaving irresponsibly. Behind the smile and carefree life of the party was an intense fear that I was going nowhere.

Did you know that your actions are a reflection of what you believe to be true about *you*? I put myself in a position to achieve exactly what I always felt was expected of me. Nothing.

Two months after I graduated from college, I was at the QVC. . .I mean CVS (I always mix those up. . .LOL), and I walked past the aisle with pregnancy tests. Besides all the unprotected sex I was having, I had *zero* reason to think for even a moment that I might be pregnant. I bought a test, took it home, and peed on the stick—or mostly peed on my hand. (I'd be doing a lot of peeing the next nine months, hint, hint.)

I waited and waited. Then I checked the box ten times like, *Okay, it's two lines and you are pregnant. But what if one is just barely visible. . .does that count? Because I feel like maybe this test is just faking me out. That can't be right. I'ma go back to CVS and splurge on the $22 digital test, because I need a more direct answer. Okay, it says yes, but could that mean yes, you are not? I feel like I need more clarification, so I'ma run back down to QVC and spend the last of my tips on the one that says "pregnant" or "not pregnant" because I need this spelled out beyond a shadow of a doubt.*

Ten tests later I couldn't stop smiling, which made no sense because I still had to tell my baby daddy.

Needless to say, my big goofy grin made no sense to him. We weren't ready to be parents. We had never even discussed marriage or children. Yet here I was, scared but with a smile on my face.

I nervously called my mom. (We laugh about it now, how I acted like I was sixteen and pregnant or something.) I was twenty-four at the time. But I was living with my rock-band boyfriend in a party house unsuitable for a baby. I made around $150 a week as a server. After I called my mom, I went out on the back porch, smoked my last cigarette, cried, laughed, and worried until I fell asleep.

Later I went to a small free Christian clinic where I was lectured about abortion. But I had only wanted to know if I was for sure pregnant and how far along I was. Honestly, I couldn't wait to get out of that clinic and away from the heat of the judgmental stares. They felt sorry for me, and I *hated* that. I hated being judged and pitied, looked down on. That was how I always felt growing up, and here I was all these years later doing exactly what I said I'd never do— becoming a young, pregnant, struggling-to-barely-get-by mama ashamed of what I just knew people thought of me.

I went into work that weekend feeling anxious and emotional. If you've ever waited tables, you know how stressful it is on a good day, let alone when you have something heavy on your heart. I never ever used trays because they scared me. My biggest fear was spilling a tray of food on customers. So I mastered the art of carrying plates on my forearms instead. I had three on one arm and two on the other. I yelled, "Corner!" and turned to walk out of the kitchen, then stepped on a really slick spot on the floor. Probably butter. Remember, this is Alabama we're talking about, so yeah, butter everywhere. I slipped *forward* and my arms were full of plates, so I couldn't catch myself. I straight up belly-flopped *into* the dining room. I was lying there on a dirty restaurant floor surrounded by shrimp and grits and broken plates, and it hit me: *this has to change.* I had to be flattened out on the floor to finally reach my all-time low. I went to the bathroom, shaky and sobbing in the handicap stall. I fell so hard that my hips were bleeding. I freaked out, not knowing if my fall could have hurt the baby. I didn't know any better. I told my manager I wanted to go home, and I cried the rest of the day.

From that day on, I took so much fuel from that fall. It's so interesting to me to that I legiterally "fell forward," because it gave me the strength to continue to "fail forward" doing whatever I needed to do to give my baby better than a mediocre life. I became so desperate for change that I couldn't continue giving the bare minimum effort at life. I needed the motivation to completely change myself, my life, and my family's future. So I went out to the thrift store, bought a pair of slacks and a blouse with an inexpensive pair of heels, and began going on interviews for a "big girl" job. I wore that outfit to every interview, because it was the only nice clothing I owned.

I ended up being hired for a "marketing" job, also known as door-to-door sales. Turned out my humor, people-reading skills, and pregnant belly made for a pretty great saleswoman. I walked up and down the streets of every Alabama town, sunup to sundown, however long it took me to earn one hundred dollars a day. Sometimes sixty to eighty hours a week. It could have been 106 degrees, a tornado, a thunderstorm, or even snow, and still I showed up and earned my money. I remember one day waddling through a thunderstorm carrying my merchandise in one arm, holding an umbrella with the other hand. The wind kept blowing the umbrella inside out, and I dropped all the coupon books I was selling. I threw the umbrella, picked up the books, found a building with an eave to stand under, squatted down soaking wet, put my head in my hands, and just sobbed. I was so tired. I was physically, mentally, and emotionally exhausted. I thought, *How can I keep this up? I'm not strong enough to get cussed out one more time today.*

I don't have a smile left to plaster onto my face. What am I gonna do? In that moment, I felt a swift kick in my tummy. My baby reminded me that what I was doing was bigger than me. My goals were greater than my soaking-wet frustration. I might give up on myself when things get tough, but I couldn't give up on her. My love for my unborn child gave me the will to keep going. So I stood up, wiped off my face, took a deep breath, and went into the next business with a laugh and a joke about how my coupons were too good to let a storm stop me. That customer bought every one!

While drenched and frustrated, I grew as a person. I learned that love is more powerful than feelings. A mother's love kept me going in the middle of a storm when my flesh was finished. Whatever you're facing in your life right now, no matter how desperate and low you feel, remember that love will never fail you. Your life has a purpose so much bigger than you. Christ's love for us was so much greater than the fear His flesh was feeling hours before He stepped into His calling on the cross. Jesus knows your pain. He knows your suffering. He felt your fears, and He cried your tears. His Spirit will give you the kick you need to keep going. I wasn't walking with Christ at that time in my life, so I didn't know it then—but, sister, I do now. It was through the lightning and thunder, and being a mother, that I grew. But it all started when I fell on my face while serving others and carrying food. Whatever trips you up will build your character when you get back up.

The qualified are called by character built in the fall.

Breaking Open My Hardened Heart

Our rock-bottom experiences are behind the most significant changes in our lives. Isn't it odd that I learned the value of life from cancer? The worst news I'd ever received led to the day I gave up my life to let God do whatever He wanted with it.

Pregnant with baby number three, I was just getting by. I was working from home, trying to hustle my way to success. Wearing myself out, losing my joy, and thinking, *I just gotta push through it. That's life. If you wanna be happy, you just gotta work harder, stay up longer—that's what it is to be a mother.* That's what I saw growing up with a single mama. Strength, perseverance, and utter exhaustion. In the midst of motherhood survival mode, I had gone into auto-pilot. The days came and went and started over again. I lived life on REPEAT. Always worried, always stressed. I didn't laugh. I didn't enjoy anything. I wasn't present in any moment. I don't even think I really knew exactly *who* I was. I cared too much about things that didn't really matter. Was trying to please everyone. (Gaaawsh, this mission impossible of people-pleasing. It sucks the joy right out of you.) I was just going through the motions when the phone rang with some news that snapped me out of mom-bie mode.

Anybody else's mom have a tendency to be the bearer of bad news? Every time my mom calls, my heart prepares for something terrible. Sometimes it's big things I need to know; other times it's to tell me that her cousin's best friend from high school died.

"Hey, babe, are you having a good day? Well, you remember Terry that I used to be friends with back in '82 before you were born? I think he held you once when you were a baby. Anyway, he died. So sad. But I gotta go, just wanted to let you know. Love you, bye."

I may have exaggerated a tiny bit to get the point across with some humor, but seriously, Mom. Quit that. (She's gonna be so mad. LOL.)

In her defense, when something happens within our family, my mom has to be the one to call and tell me. We have a tiny little bunch of family at this point, and I'm fourteen hours away from them. So that's just another thing a mother does. Tells us the hard things, even though she hates to see us hurting.

Well, during this call, my mom was letting me know that my niece Ansley wasn't feeling well, and my sister Cassie was taking her to the emergency room. Probably to get her tonsils taken out. She wanted to keep me in the loop. Ansley had just turned six years old. A few days before, I was looking at pictures of her running around at the park. I had no idea she had been having trouble swallowing and breathing at night. She'd had allergies since she was a toddler, but her antibiotics didn't seem to be working anymore. My sister was getting really concerned, so she decided to take Ansley to the emergency room.

I went about my day thinking everything would be fine. We all have kids, and things happen all the time, and everyone always ended up being okay. But when my mom called me back about an hour later, before I even answered the phone I got the worst feeling in my gut. When I answered, I could tell by the way my mom uttered, "Hey, babe," that something was wrong. She had such an obvious tone of worry, and I could tell she was trying to tamp down her own emotion to deliver the news to me. Ansley had just been diagnosed with cancer.

In that moment, everything stopped. The earth stopped spinning. My heart stopped beating. I put down the phone, went to the bathroom, locked the door, and paced back and forth trying to control my emotions. Trying not to freak out, because I was seven months pregnant, and this diagnosis didn't necessarily mean Ansley was dying. *But does this mean she's dying? No, we don't know that. I don't know anything. I'm so far away. I need to go. I gotta go.* As panic took over, so did my tears. I fell to the floor and just began sobbing. Sobbing so hard that I couldn't breathe or move. Then I thought about my sister and, as a mother, I felt what was left of my heart shatter. I thought, *I have to get to her. I need to be there.* I called my ob-gyn to see if I was cleared to fly. I was having a perfect, healthy pregnancy, so she wrote me a note and let me go.

When I arrived, my mom filled me in on exactly what had happened. Cassie was worried that something other than allergies was causing Ansley to have such a hard time breathing, especially at night. When she went to the emergency room, the doctor there said she wasn't sure what my sister wanted her to do if it was just allergies. Cassie told me she actually said, "I don't know what you want me to do." But an EMT, who had looked into Ansley's throat, spoke up and said he thought he saw something. So the doctor took Ansley back for an X-ray.

When the doctor came back, she looked at my sister and asked, "Do you know what Saint Jude is?" My sister told me she just responded, "No. No. She just needs her tonsils taken out. That's what we came for. It's her tonsils."

The doctor explained that Ansley had two walnut-sized tumors right behind her facial palate. They were growing rapidly down into her throat. They needed to get from Huntsville, Alabama, to Saint Jude in Memphis immediately. They went in for tonsils and left with cancer. Nobody even had time to comprehend what was happening. They didn't go home and get clothes and figure out next steps. They went straight to Saint Jude where Ansley immediately went into surgery. While in surgery, the doctors were unable to get a tube down her throat, so they ended up having to do an emergency tracheotomy so she could breathe. This poor child woke up with a hole in her throat, a box in her chest, and a feeding tube in her stomach. Her little body underwent so much stress in such a short time that she almost died. They were in the recovery room, and my sister said machines just started beeping and going off, and before they knew it doctors and nurses filled the room pushing them aside. They stood in the back, completely helpless and terrified, watching as the Saint Jude staff did all they could to revive my niece. It must have seemed like an eternity before her numbers returned to normal and she started breathing again.

By the time I got to the hospital, I'm pretty sure my sister was operating on nothing but a mother's protective adrenaline. She has no idea just how inspired I am by her strength. She was hurting so badly, but she didn't let Ansley see her own worry, fear, and heartbreak. My niece was probably in a bit of shock herself. She wasn't showing much emotion or reaction to anyone. I didn't even see her cry. It was like she just took it. The next day we took Ansley's hair down and tried our best to comb through the knots and tangles. We played Connect Four, and I got a small grin from her. But the best thing that happened that day was my sister getting to hold Ansley for the first time since everything had happened. The nurses were trying to help her get up and get moving. They wanted her to try to walk and use the bathroom on her own. Ansley was absolutely terrified to move. So before they put her back in bed, they let her sit in Cassie's lap. When my sister wrapped her arms around her baby girl for the first time since they had arrived at Saint Jude (rocking her, comforting her, and kissing her head), without shedding a single tear, I realized that she is the strongest woman I will ever know. It is such a selfless kind of caring that can restrain emotion at a time like that. Her need to soothe her daughter was greater than her sorrow. That's a mother's love.

(I'm not crying, you're crying. This is tough to read, I know. It's tough to write. Let's get through this, though, because it's a story that needs to be shared.)

Ansley was moved into isolation to continue her recovery from surgery. Cassie and JR (my brother-in-law) learned Ansley had a rare form of childhood cancer called rhabdomyosarcoma, RMS for short. The doctors created an aggressive treatment plan since it is a rapidly growing cancer. So not only would Ansley undergo seven surgeries, but she'd soon begin "treatment." She was pretty depressed and often lay on her side under her blanket, staring off sadly. She couldn't really talk because of the trach. The music girl, Amy, came in with a guitar and some instruments. She asked if she could sing Ansley a song. AA (Ansley's nickname) nodded. She began to play "Roar" by Katy Perry. The spirit in the room grew heavy as we stood back, watching her sing those powerful words to a tiny, terrified little girl in for the fight of her life. We all began to choke up, but it was at this moment that my sister finally allowed herself to feel a little bit of what was happening. She stepped into the bathroom, closed the door, and cried her heart out. When the song was over and Amy asked if she'd like another, Ansley tapped on the tambourine. It was the first time she had responded to anyone for a couple of days. We were all so happy to see her interact, even if it was just a flick of her wrist. Ansley really needed Amy the music lady that day. She gave her a tiny lift of the spirit. And we all felt it.

During this time, I felt pretty useless. I was so happy to watch over AA while my sister and JR got some desperately needed sleep a few nights. Ansley let me tickle her palm while we watched movies and I read to her. But I really missed her smile. The one thing I was always good at was getting a giggle from her, even at the toughest of times. Ansley's room had an automatic door since she was in isolation. I noticed her door would kind of malfunction sometimes, and one day it almost closed on one of the nurses. Ansley accidentally let a tiny laugh slip through her lips. She quickly took it back and reverted to her mad face. But I knew I had her. . . . A few minutes later, I got up to walk out and in true exaggerated fashion, I acted like I couldn't get through the door. Like the door was trying to get me on purpose. So I did a little dance with it and let it shut on my leg, tripping me up as I tumbled out of the room. Ansley about busted a gut, cackling. Then I walked over by the small window to the little outside room and acted like I was taking the elevator, and then like I was tripping down the stairs. A huge grin lit up her face.

I stayed in Memphis for nearly a week and then had to return home, or I would have been too pregnant to fly. When I told Ansley goodbye, she got really upset with me. I wish I could have stayed with her. Saying goodbye, knowing what she was about to endure, was one of the hardest things I've ever had to do. I told her how much I loved her and how strong I knew she was. I kissed her face, held her hand, and promised I'd see her again soon. Then I forced myself to turn and walk away from her. From Ansley, my sister, my mom, and our whole family. I wouldn't be able to see them until Christmas, and it wrecked me.

I didn't cry the entire time I was there. Not even in the airport when I received an invasive full-body pat-down because the radiation set the wand off. . .or when my flight got delayed twice. It was the next day, after I dropped my girls off at school and pulled into my garage. I kept thinking of Ansley's face when I said goodbye, all the things Cassie and JR were facing, the other children and babies I saw there, and the worst thought of all: *What if she doesn't make it?* It was then, alone in my car, that I broke. Completely fell apart. I wasn't praying. I actually hadn't prayed at all the whole time in Memphis. I was not searching for answers or begging for healing. I was just mindlessly sobbing uncontrollably, totally overwhelmed with grief.

I wasn't looking for God. But I was brokenhearted enough that day to recognize Him. Out of nowhere,

I felt warmth and peace wash over me. My tears slowed, and I could breathe again. I felt overwhelming love and relief. I knew without a doubt that I wasn't alone, and I knew exactly who was with me. Psalm 34:18 says God is near to the brokenhearted. I truly believe it's because when your heart is broken, so is your connection to all the worldly things that have been clouding your spirit's vision.

We don't find God. He isn't lost. We are. He's always there, seeking us out. We *realize* He is there and *recognize* Him when everything else is removed and we are humbled. Someone I loved more than myself was suffering, and I had zero pride in the way. I didn't say a word. I just closed my eyes and felt the calm in my soul. Three words came into my spirit: *"Give it up."*

And I knew what those words meant. I had been fighting the truth for a very long time. I needed to hand over my life and let go of control. I needed to die to myself and let my life serve God for the good of others. So, completely defeated, I simply said, "Okay."

I went on, "Take it. Take it, Lord. Take my heart, take my life, take my chains, take my mistakes, and take my pain. I will *let* You have it. I'll lay it down at Your feet, and I will walk away and let You use it to mold me into a servant for whatever is my purpose.

I'll do whatever You tell me to do."

I kid you not, God said, "*Speak.*"

Say what? What do You mean, "Speak"? I know I just said I'd do whatever You wanted, but like, is this a test?

Y'all know most people would rather *die* than speak publicly, right? This was the beginning of a friendship between the Lord and me, as well as the connection I have with the Holy Spirit. It's personal. It's an intimate relationship. A relationship founded on love. A love that I wasn't ready to receive until my walls were down. It was a love that accepted me for who I am and showed me exactly who I was created to be. A love that revealed to me all the many ways God has always been there watching over me, hurting with me, understanding me, and growing me. For someone who hadn't read a ton of the Bible, I began to really understand what it was that Jesus did for me—for *all* of us—and why. I began to realize that God wasn't ready and waiting to punish me for being imperfect; instead, He was ready and waiting for me to let Him use my uniqueness for the good of others as well as for the good plans He always had for me.

And, sister, the same is true for you. If you are reading this and going through something that seems too heavy for you to carry, let Him have it. The rocks tied to your feet are dragging you to the bottom, making it hard for you to breathe. Let Him set you free. You can be weak—that's when you see His strength. Be humble and meek. Lay your burdens down at His feet. Let Jesus take the driver's seat.

Have trust and faith, because without them, how well are things going in your life? Living according to what I thought was best wasn't working out very well for me. It left me overwhelmed and confused most of the time. I needed discernment and guidance. Life hadn't exactly been fabulous without Him. At least with Him when things really, *really* suck, I can feel peace, love, joy, and strength when most people would not.

That's where Jesus shines through. People feel uncomfortable and confused seeing someone who can live with joy in the midst of tragedy. You can't blend in with the world when you're not the average girl. You are a daughter of the King with an ability to overcome your feelings. That's not human nature. You can feel joy when times are sad, be glad when you should be mad, and show love to people who have treated you bad. The absolute worst year of my life led to a realization that saved my life. My rock-bottom experience brought me to revelation. That's how life works. Oddly enough.

If you're ready with your tissues, turn the page and you'll come to understand how my niece's life led to you reading this book right now.

CHAPTER 4

Painful Purpose

Praise be to the God and Father of our Lord Jesus Christ, the Father of compassion and the God of all comfort, who comforts us in all our troubles, so that we can comfort those in any trouble with the comfort we ourselves receive from God.

2 CORINTHIANS 1:3–4

I finally let go and gave my life up to God that day in my car, alone in my garage. I walked into my house a different person than when I had pulled into the driveway crushed and brokenhearted. The first thing God said to me was, *"Speak."* I didn't know what it meant at first, so to start I just began telling everyone I possibly could what had happened in my car. I didn't even realize at the time that I was sharing my testimony. I told everyone that God told me I was going to speak and so somehow, some way, that was what I was going to do. People looked at me like I was a little crazy, because who just decides out of nowhere that they are going to be a public speaker?

And so the self-doubt began to creep in. The "Who do you think you are?" thoughts. But every time, I thought of my niece—my inspiration—who was in the fight of her life. I thought about how young she was, how much potential she had that might never be realized. I imagined how badly she wanted to do the simplest things we take for granted. Like wake up in her own bed, go to school, dance, play, and just be a child. She physically could not do the things with her life that she wanted. She was fighting through chemo, radiation, braces on her legs, isolation, throwing up, losing all of her hair, burns on her face, ulcers in the lining of her stomach, and just trying to survive. I had *nothing* stopping me from pursuing God's calling on my life. So I would— because I trusted Him. I believed Him.

I decided to do something positive each day in Ansley's honor. So I began sharing her story. Letting people know the truths about childhood cancer and how it was impacting our family. I made sure to include the part where I finally gave it all up to God. I started pouring into myself as much as I could. I found a motivational speaker named Les Brown on YouTube and started listening to him every day while pretending to clean, working out, or driving. His videos led me to other speakers like Eric Thomas (*It's ya boooy ET!*), Joyce Meyer, and Priscilla Shirer. In the beginning I couldn't really understand how listening to these people could actually change someone's life. But over time, I realized it's not the videos that change your life; it's the impact these speakers' words have on your thoughts each day that then, over time, become your actions. So if you pour uplifting, empowering, inspiring, encouraging words into your brain each day, your actions will begin to be those of a person with hope, purpose, aspirations, belief, and determination. What you tell yourself will be reflected in your actions. Hearing Joyce Meyer speak of her past sexual abuse, tell jokes, and use what she has been through to reach others really inspired me to let it all loose on anyone who would listen. Joyce became a role model for me—showing how someone like me could be used massively for His glory.

Sister, if you tell yourself each day that you are worthless, ugly, tired, and stupid, it's no wonder you don't take care of yourself or have a good attitude. No wonder you don't put much effort into your life. No wonder you aren't happy. What you believe about yourself *will* be the life you live. I've never seen anyone hate themselves into a happy, healthy life—have you? It wasn't until I *felt* God's love for me that I was able to truly love who He made me to be.

I have to work on this daily. I battle all kinds of negative thoughts each day. I have caught my reflection in the full-length mirror before getting in the shower—the "bent over and naked" angle is not the most flattering. Especially when your boobs have gone from an A to an F within an hour. Three kids sucked the life right out of them. One day I was walking into the Targets and dang near turned around and went home to exchange my shorts for pants because I saw so much cellulite on my thighs.

When I say, "Ladies, stop hating your body," I'm talking to myself as well. Your body is a reflection of how you treat it. It's doing the best it can to get you through this life, despite the many ways you may abuse it. Don't hate your body for the marks left by the stretching it did when your baby grew inside it. It's okay not to love your body every day. We all have days when self-love just isn't showing up. But always come back to what's important. Put forth the effort to remind yourself as often as possible that your health, and the health and safety of those you love, matters. When you look in the mirror today—yes, *today*—I want you to look at your body and make it a promise. Promise to love it and care for it the same way you take care of everything else you hold dear to your heart. If you have a sickness or disease, then promise to help it along the best you can.

Self-love will help you have joy throughout the journey and be at peace. Self-hate has driven many to look a certain way—but when hating your body serves as your inspiration, you'll never be satisfied. You will always find something else wrong with your body. Don't you want to be at peace with yourself? Not just physically, but mentally and emotionally? I want you to be happy. I want you to love yourself now so that you can maintain your health and fulfill God's calling on your life—so you can pass that joy on to others. It's hard to be a vessel when you're sick and miserable. Have you ever wished your children would see themselves the way you see them? I want the same for you—I want you to see what God sees in you. You are beautiful. You are strong. You are worthy. You are loved.

I know. . .that was a squirreled-out tangent, but I'm leaving it because you need to know how awesome you are, and if more women began to truly love themselves, we could come together and change the whole dang world.

Ansley's sickness gave me a new perspective on my own health, and the most important thing I've learned is that health starts with how you think about and speak to yourself. For over a year, this became my focus: to love God, love others, love myself, keep trying and trusting. God is good, and He has a plan for me. I said those words all day, every day. God placed all kinds of promises and vision into my heart, but instead of worrying about how I was going to get there or trying to force it to happen quickly, I just had to wake up each day and try my best to stay on the path He set before me. It took effort not to let the enemy sideline and distract me; staying in a good headspace was absolutely necessary.

Ansley did have improvements at times, but each day was unknown. Cancer is a living cell, so it will fight to survive, and it moves and changes. It can even outsmart treatment sometimes. For Ansley's birthday I decided to post a video on Facebook singing to her as silly as possible. It was to make her smile. That smile was worth any potential criticism I'd receive. She helped bring my goofy back, and so did the personal development. When you find yourself again, you gain the ability to think and speak freely. I found the crazy, sarcastic, silly side of myself and made a decision to let it be seen. If I could make Ansley laugh, it didn't matter what anyone else thought. This mind-set helped me reconnect with the happiness I felt making others laugh. A moment of laughter can help all your worries fade. And I remembered how I loved being that distraction for people.

I didn't see my niece in person again until Christmas. She was able to come home from Saint Jude for the holidays. It was eight months after her diagnosis. She couldn't walk at this point, because the cancer had moved to her spinal fluid. She was also on steroids, so her face was really swollen. It was tough to see her like that. I can't imagine how my sister and brother-in-law must have felt. She got to hold my baby, Bodie, for the first time. We went to Build-A-Bear where everyone stared as we slowly carried her through, holding up the line. She smiled in all the pictures, even though she was clearly sad that she couldn't run around and play with her cousins like she always had before. My oldest daughter was very close to her, and she was sad to see her cousin like that. My kids hadn't realized just how sick Ansley was until they saw her in person. Saying goodbye completely broke my heart. AA was so sad for us to leave. I tried hard not to cry in front of her, but I had a horrible feeling it might be the last time I wrapped my arms around her. We live fourteen hours away, so I was fighting thoughts that the next time I came home it would be to say our final goodbyes. Or even worse, that this *was* our final goodbye.

I don't think there are words to describe how devastating it feels to give a hug to a child you love as if they were your own with a fear that it might be the very last. I could barely get myself to leave Ansley's side. About four months later, the cancer spread to her brain, and the doctors at Saint Jude felt like continued treatment would only make the remainder of her life harder. She was released to be comfortable in her own home for the rest of her time. Our family held on to the possibility of a miracle, but I was also completely aware that the miracle might have been the time we were already given in her presence.

Three months after Ansley's release from Saint Jude, her brain tumor was so large that one of her eyes was almost completely closed, and she often didn't make sense when she spoke. I was shocked how clearly she talked when she FaceTimed us. Ansley asked me to pass the iPad to each one of my daughters, back and forth, just to tell them over and over again how much she loved them. That's all she kept saying: "I love you, Presley. Let me see Kansas. I love you, Kansas. I love you. I love you. I love you." She just wanted all of us to know how much she loved us. My mom said Ansley had asked for me several times and that they didn't think it would be long, so I scheduled a flight to get to her as quickly as I could.

The next morning we were getting ready to walk out the door to go to the airport when the phone rang. My husband answered it, sat down on the couch, and just said, "Oh, man." He looked at me with a defeated expression, and my heart sank. She was gone. She had taken her last breath in my sister's bed, wrapped in her mother's arms, and everyone was overcome with grief. I had to go to the airport with my two daughters and get on a plane, having just been given the news that I would never speak to my seven-year-old niece again. After such a long, hard fight. For a while, it really killed me that I didn't make it in time to tell her goodbye. That she had asked for me and I wasn't there. But I know it is better that I don't have that memory to carry with me. It's not as peaceful an exit as people imagine it to be. She struggled for her last breath. For my sister, my brother-in-law, and my other niece, Lacy, it was anything but peaceful. It was their time with her—it was their time to cry out, hold her body, beg her to stay, and then watch completely crushed as she was taken away. My daughters and I didn't need to be there for that final moment. I know that now.

Not once have I felt angry with God over this loss. But I don't blame those who have been angry with Him. Overwhelming grief can't be understood or explained, and everyone processes it differently. Losing a loved one is probably the number one strain on a person's faith.

But I had an understanding that day in my car—not only was I loved, but so were my niece and my sister and our whole family. And while God's love doesn't always protect us from all the evil in the world, it does help us conquer it. We conquer it through what we choose to do with our own lives and how we spend our time. We defeat it by loving others. One of my favorite songs by Hillsong United, "Heaven Knows," has a message that sticks with me: the greatest act of love humankind has ever known revealed itself through sacrifice, tears, blood, and pain. It was so powerful that it conquered death. It's the love we've given to those we've lost that makes us hurt so deeply. And it's the love that dripped from Jesus' wrists that gives us strength to keep moving forward through our pain.

I know my life will be full of pain because we live in a fallen world—a world where evil does exist. When I feel angry, I direct my anger at the enemy, and I despise him enough to notice the beauty in things that break my heart. Nothing makes me happy dance more than reflecting on a moment in my life that could have killed me, a moment the enemy specifically orchestrated, and then using it for God's glory. And I believe this was always Ansley's story. The outcome played out just the way it was supposed to. You know what inspires me so much about my family? Even though none of us understand *why* Ansley got sick, we still love God. And so does my sister. In fact, she gives me so much inspiration through her determination to keep moving forward. She is walking, talking, and breathing each day, all with a giant hole in her heart. I love her and my family so much. We have been through many hard things, but we will not be broken. We still laugh.

After Ansley's funeral, we returned to my sister's house and pulled out our favorite game, Aggravation. We sat around the kitchen table, rolling the dice, moving the marbles, and, yes, laughing. Now and then it would get quiet and Ansley's absence would sit heavily in our hearts. But we kept rolling the dice, and the game continued.

There will never be a family get-together or holiday where each of us isn't hyperaware of who is missing. In the midst of the giggles of my girls and Lacy, there's a deafening silence where Ansley's laughter once was. And it hurts. It hurts every day. The truth is, we grieve for ourselves. We grieve for the pain we feel living in a world where she isn't physically present. We want her here. We grieve for what she went through. Even though we know she's experiencing a level of love and peace she could never know here in the world, and we know we will see her again, it still hurts. Nothing can change that. So if I'm going to feel this pain anyway, I've decided to go ahead and do something with it. The more I hurt, the harder I'm gonna love. The greater my grief, the better it feels to make someone giggle. If you're hurting, either you can pay that hurt forward by hurting others, or you can allow yourself to heal by helping others.

Three months after Ansley passed away, I was asked to speak at my first small women's event. I desperately wanted to say no. But when God puts an open door in front of my face, I don't have a choice. There is no choice. And so I say yes, especially when the only reason I want to say no is fear. Fear is the greatest indicator to me that it's a God thing. His calling on your life is so much bigger than you that it's difficult to accept that it could be real. So fear creeps in to try to prevent you from doing what your mind perceives as a threat.

I always pray for discernment to know when something is a God thing, and most of the time my spirit can tell it is if it makes me nervous. Nervousness is a good indicator that you are about to step into your purpose. Unless you're about to step into a creepy dark alley all alone late at night. Then it's a response to an actual threat and you need to run away. Just sprint away, wildly flailing arms and all, screaming, "Help me, Jesus!" while spraying some mace behind you—just in case. That's what I would do, and I've never been chased...so it must work.

At the conference, I sat in the pew trying to

control my nerves, waiting to be called up front to share. I couldn't get my heart to slow down, and I could feel myself sweating. My hands were so wet it was hard to even hold on to the microphone. As I stood up in front of everyone, I wondered if they could see how badly I was shaking and if they could hear how afraid I was. I had nothing—and I mean *nothing*—planned. Yes, I know that sounds ridiculous. But I scored a perfect 100 in junior college for one class. Speech. True story. I would research a topic and just go up and talk about it. I never wrote anything down. My teacher told me I needed to go into something like broadcasting, and I just laughed it off like she was a crazy person. So, as with many other things I think I can do just like when I was young (run, stay up late, eat whatever I want, look cute in a romper), I figured it would be as easy now as it was then. When I got done delivering what I felt was a blubbering mess of a speech, I felt strangely exhilarated. I was genuinely surprised how many people told me that my words really touched their hearts. I didn't think anything I said even made sense. But turns out, when God takes over, people tend to hear exactly what they need to hear. I knew in that moment that there's absolutely nothing I—nothing *you*—can't do if it's God's purpose. I went home on cloud nine, already wondering when I'd get to speak again.

I wanted to share, share, share.

But God is always working to help me give Him control. And He does this by making me be still and wait. So six months later, I participated in a "dance like nobody's watching" challenge. In an effort to be really, *really* real, I decided to go for it. The exact way I do when the only people home are my kids and me. While I was recording a workout, the song "Push It" by Salt-N-Pepa came on. If you don't drop what you're doing and break it down like a drunken college student (as the meme says) when this song comes on, we can't be friends. I went for it. I just let it all out. Funky facial expressions and *errrrrythang*. My kids in the background, whining and fussing over the iPad, and all the mom-life realness right there on video. When I watched it back, I cackled. But I hesitated to post it. I mean, I was twerking in sweatpants, wearing a headband that said "Mommin' Ain't Easy," *and* I choked on my spit halfway through and nearly died. But there was that voice—the one that can't be ignored, urging me to post the video.

Yes, y'all. God told me to post a video twerking to a not-so-Christian song. I don't know what to tell ya. Jesus loves using sinners for His work. I posted the video on my personal Facebook page and ran away. About an hour later my mom called. "Carolanne, I thank that video you posted is going viral." Y'all I got so scared. I was like, *Nooooooo.* Not twerking with the stank face and choking on my spit in front of errrybody like that. *Please, God, say it isn't so.* I got online and saw it had eight thousand views. And just an hour later it had nearly thirty thousand. My mom called me again. "Yer gonna be on *Ellen!*" People were blowing up my phone with comments like, "I just saw a video of you dancing on my friend's page—she doesn't even know you." I freaked out, turned off my phone, and went to bed.

The next day the video had more than a million views. I have never seen any viral video—no matter how innocent it was—*not* have a bunch of people in the comment threads saying horrible things. And I certainly never expected to be the one on the receiving end. So I had a choice to make. I could let the fear of people's reactions overwhelm me and hide under a rock until it blew over. Or I could embrace the promise God made me when Ansley got sick. I had a "fan" page for my health/fitness coaching that I didn't really use that much. It had three hundred pity follows from friends and family. So I posted the dance video over there, thinking there was no way it would receive the same attention as it did on my personal page. It would just be insane for the video to go viral twice in a week from two different pages, right?

Welp, through God all things are possible, because it hit a million views in less than twenty-four hours, and my page went from three hundred followers to twenty-five thousand *overnight*. I can't even. The video now has about three million views from my personal page and almost thirty million views from the page many of you know me from today, CA Miljavac.

Not long after the first viral video, live feeds became a thing, and just like that a platform was born. I could speak. And I was terrified. But I had promised God that if He gave me a platform, I'd give Him the glory. I knew it might cost me popularity at times, but I didn't care. Ansley's story had to be shared. Her story needed to be shared with other hurting hearts and all the people out there like me. Two years later with thirty viral videos, over 100 million views, and nearly half a million followers, I am sitting here writing this book you now hold in your hands.

So, you see, there's purpose in all of our pain. And oddly enough, *you* are a part of my purpose. I know it's hard to grapple with emotions and struggles, and I know it's hard to believe there's a good God out there who loves you and has a calling on your life. But I promise you, if you shut out the world and believe what He says about you, there is *nothing* He can't do with your future. *Nothing.* If He can take this poor, abused, abandoned, bullied, broken-hearted little hick out of the trailer park in the country and up to the podium speaking for His glory, He can use you as a vessel too.

I am so far from perfect. I am not holier than thou. I'm not always wholesome and sunshine with rainbow sprinkles. My flesh is full of anger, and I wanna punch people in the face sometimes. I can be defensive and full of doubt. I have a hard time saying I'm sorry to my husband even when I know I should. But as I am, I am loved. As you are, you are loved. It's what you can be that God sees.

And yet, I still grieve.

But you know what I love about grieving with Jesus? I don't have to fake it. I don't have to shove it down and pretend just to get through the day. I can feel it. I can feel every last jab, stick, and stab of grief in my heart and still recover. And *when* I recover, I'll have a new tool in my box for the good of others. You have to *feel* it in order to lay it down so He can heal it. If you won't let your pain come to the surface, it will forever remain as a seed of self-destruction inside your heart.

You can't bring the pain you won't acknowledge to the altar. There's no room for pride when it comes to pain, and there's no shame in crying. Strength is found in weakness. It takes a great show of trust in the Holy Spirit to allow yourself to crumble. Many times we stifle our tears for fear we won't be able to stop them once they start. But God can't make you whole in your weakness if you won't admit you've been broken. So you really have to trust that when you let go, He will send the Holy Spirit to fill the holes in your heart. When your trust is broken, along with your heart, it's tough to let go. He *understands*. He knows, y'all. He knows what you're feeling, and He feels it too.

So when you need to be angry, when you question God and sling plates at His head, He's not mad at ya for it. He is ready and waiting—with open arms—for you to be done with your grief so He can step in and help you move forward.

———

Sometimes I feel like we play this game of "Who has it worse?" I see people do it all the time—compare their hardships to others'. Deep down, sometimes I think we want ours to be the worst so nobody will challenge us to live a better life. Who would step in and tell a grieving mother that she can still use her life and her child's life to serve a greater purpose? Who would tell an abused child that God can work that out for their good?

As adults we form quite the relationship with our pain. It can become a security blanket and an excuse to live in a way that's destroying us. If that's you, I'm telling you that no matter what you've been through, someone is suffering just as much—if not more—and whether you like it or not, Jesus suffered it too. And you are still here. Your life has a purpose. Quit using your grief as a reason to live in mediocre misery. Haven't you noticed that the most impactful, inspiring people in the world have lived through an intense amount of hardship? They got through it just like you will get through it. Yes, you will get through it. Getting through it may not look like you want it to, but you are *here*. You are *still here*.

If you're still reading, deep down you know that if you have breath in your lungs, there's potential in your life. Hopeless people sure as heck don't read personal-growth books. But getting through a hardship doesn't always mean getting past it. You may have put your emotions in PARK because you refuse to dig up your pain and deal—which means your pain serves no purpose, and you are stuck in a rut.

You *choose* what you're going to do with what you go through. Working through grief is hard; wallowing in it is easy. Three important pieces of the process are *accept, acknowledge,* and *allow*.

It's so hard to accept what you're experiencing at first. To take it and own it. So some of us live in a state of denial that leaves us unable to grow from what we have been given. When I say *given*, I don't necessarily mean God gave it to you either. When Ansley was diagnosed with cancer, God didn't give her that. He knew what would happen. He knew she'd get sick and what we would go through. So He allows hardship, yes, but doesn't always cause it. I had to accept that I was molested. That my dad didn't know how to be a dad. That my niece is no longer present in this world. Bad things happen. People hurt each other. Struggles will come. I accept that I'm not immune to suffering. I also accept that, despite all those things, I'm loved.

Are there times when we have to undergo a difficult experience to become what we need to be for God's calling on our lives? Absolutely. But sometimes we go through things as a culmination of factors, trickled down from all kinds of different sources. Environment (wildfires destroying neighborhoods), consequences of our actions (jail time as a result of drugs), ripple effects of the decisions of other people we may not even know (the person on drugs who broke into your car), timing (being in a bank when someone decided to rob it), and the list goes on. We live in a world where evil exists among people with free will. And like it or not, we brought imperfection into the world and not one of us can escape the struggle and grief that come with it. But we can allow the Holy Spirit to do exactly what Christ meant for Him to do: to provide guidance, knowledge, purpose, discernment, joy, strength, and peace in the midst of life's ups and downs.

If we can grow spiritually to a point of acknowledging the truth—that no matter how hurt we are, God still loves us—it will be possible to allow Him inside our weak spots so He can give us His strength. Our time on earth is given to us for the purpose of a beautiful experience—time to love and laugh. Discover what it's like to live with a tiny taste of the Creator's vision. You are the greatest part of His vision. Acknowledge who you are. Say out loud: "I'm loved. I'm enough. I'm not alone. I have gifts. There's a purpose for me." Even if you feel dirty or unworthy, you are just as breathtaking to Him now as the day you were born. According to Deuteronomy 31:6, nothing can change that. He will never leave you or forsake you.

Do you have kids? Is there anything they could do to erase the way you saw them from the very day they were born? I will always be head over heels in love with my kids and all the potential they have. I know they are going to make mistakes, no matter how much guidance I give them. When they ask for milk, then say they really wanted water, then complain because the water isn't milk. . .I love them anyway. My arms will always be open to them when they need reassurance, a place to cry, forgiveness, or cuddles. And God's arms will always be open to you. Even when He gives you more than you ask for, and you still aren't happy. Even when you get mad because He doesn't give you what you want, because it's not what you need. My toddler wants to play in the street, but she can't see the cars coming like I can. God knows more than we do, and He loves us, so we must give up control for trust.

Sister, the beauty of life lives in you. It lives in your joy. It lives in your laugh. It lives in your gifts and in your talents. If you've given your life to Him, Christ lives in you. Don't let the world shut out the part of you that can change the world—the part of you that is superhuman. It's the part of you that makes no sense to those who don't have faith in Jesus. It's the part of you that stirs up curiosity. It separates you from the rest. What makes you stand out is the way you navigate through the same ups and downs, trauma, strife, and struggles that everyone else has, but with an unusual spirit of peace. The peace that surpasses all understanding (see Philippians 4:7). I'll happily be the weirdo if it means joy through my struggles. If the majority are hateful and unhappy, I'd much rather be the outcast. Look around. The world is overwhelmed with sin. I don't want to fit in. Do you? Can I get an amen?

When we feel the depths of grief squeezing the air from our lungs and our tears fog up our vision, it's okay to wonder where our good, good Father has gone. We aren't supposed to understand. We aren't capable of seeing past our own emotions in times of loss and suffering. A loved one's absence can simply be just too much for our hearts to handle at times. Wounds take time to heal. We need to be angry with someone when nothing makes sense. Blame is a basket: we can pour our emotion into it just to get it off our chest. It's necessary to feel whatever it is you are feeling in whatever stage of grief you're in. If you don't feel it, you can't heal it. You cannot heal if you won't deal. You gotta cry until the tears run dry. You gotta sob until your only option is to move on. No pain is so deep as a loved one's absence. If you try to hide it away, it will morph into self-destruction and the devil wins. But he can't have your soul if you've decided to follow Jesus; however, he can easily take away your joy with his hooks in your grieving.

As you know, my sister has suffered what many would consider an impossible-to-recover-from loss. She didn't just lose her baby girl. She watched her suffer, while hope dangled just out of reach for over a year. She lost Ansley slowly over time, completely helpless to do anything about it. Reminds me of Mary and how she watched as her boy had the flesh violently ripped from His bones. She helplessly witnessed as He was beaten, spit on, and mocked, as He had nails driven through His flesh and suffered in horrific pain so that the very same people who killed Him could have a chance at salvation.

Some of you have suffered such loss that you catch yourself struggling in your faith. You have had thoughts like, *How can a loving God allow such horrible things to happen to good people? What kind of God lets His children suffer like this?* The answer is and always will be this: the kind of God who allowed His Son the free will to choose to save you from the clutches of Satan. He wants you to love Him because you choose to. Not because He forces you to. In the beginning, He provided a world free from cruelty, sickness, evil, and sin. He gave us the gift of experiencing life on earth with only good plans for us—even still, with free will. We were never meant to know everything. And we aren't guaranteed a life without suffering. I know I'm not promised tomorrow, and neither are the people I love. But when you are hurting, never forget that the way to recover is to go out and do good for others. That's the purpose in your pain. Oddly enough.

CHAPTER 5

HiDE-AND-SEEK

"You did not choose me, but I chose you and appointed you so that you might go and bear fruit—fruit that will last—and so that whatever you ask in my name the Father will give you."

JOHN 15:16

When I was little and we were at the Walmarts (it's a southern thing), I loved sneaking off to hide from my mama. I would climb in the middle of the clothes rack and peek out through the shirts when she walked by. When I dodged her successfully, I'd giggle at how sneaky I was. Like, *Wow, I'm practically ninja material.* Sometimes I'd stick my hand out and touch her arm to freak her out. I'd watch her from afar and try to get from aisle to aisle without her seeing me. The grand finale was always an epic scare. I would tiptoe up behind her or grab her hand when she reached to take a shirt off my hideout rack. My mom actually knew exactly where I was and what I was doing, but I think she got a kick out of making me believe she couldn't see me. Even when she told me she could see me, I would just argue with her. I was Chuck Norris, and she just couldn't admit that I got her good. (This was back in the day when kids used their imaginations.) It's no wonder Mama used to make us stay in the car. Yes, that used to be no big deal. All three of us kids would stay in the car and try not to kill each other or break a window before she got back.

You know, just like I couldn't hide from my mama, you can't hide from your heavenly Father. No matter how much sin hangs on your hideout rack, He sees you. No mistake is big enough to block you from His sight. There were times in my life I really thought our family accidentally got overlooked. Everything was hard. The simplest things. Even grocery shopping. Do you know what it feels like to be looked down on in public? I could see the anxiety grow on my mom's face as each grocery item beeped across the scanner. I could tell she was on pins and needles waiting to see if her card would go through. I would feel just as nervous. But it was the looks on the faces of the people in line that made me want to disappear. My mom would remove items we needed the least and swipe the card—again—hoping eventually it would go through. Sometimes it would work, and we'd leave with our milk, bread, cheese, tuna, and ground beef. Other days we would have to walk away from an entire buggy of food. I felt so. . .poor. I despised the looks of pity. I hated the eye rolls and sighs as we held up the line.

From the time I was about eight years old, I began to feel very defensive of my family. *We don't need your pity, and we don't need your help.* I wanted to take people down a notch. And anger began to settle into my core. I was angry with people for thinking they were better than us. I was angry with my mama for not having money. I was angry with God. Mama had begun to take us to church by this point in my life. She drove by Northside Baptist and couldn't shake the feeling that we needed to be there. Dragged us there three times a week. She prayed, and she sang. She gave her life to Jesus. But here we were in line at the Walmarts once again, walking away from food and disapproving stares.

So. . .why, God? Why aren't You making things better? Why do we have to keep struggling so much? Where's this good plan everyone keeps saying You have for us? Because my mama's still cryin' at night, we still have little to nothing, and I'm still hungry. Starving for any life other than this one. Do we just not matter? I see so many people around me with everything they need. Do You just not see us? How many more prayers does my mama need to pray before we see change?

With every judgmental stare as the years passed, the anger I felt grew deeper and deeper. It started revealing itself through self-destruction. I started getting *such* an attitude with my mom—all the time. Mean jokes, sarcasm, hateful tones, and eye rolls so deep they actually made me dizzy. I was rebellious. *Obviously, God's not seeing us, so why do I care about trying so hard to follow all these rules? Look how much good it's doing my mom.* I just stopped caring. My grades were only ever high enough to play softball; I used my humor to be the class clown at the expense of my dignity; and I decided to be a wild child down for anything. *I'll be cool. Nobody will laugh at me unless it's my intention.* I'd lean on "friends" for acceptance, and the church could keep their opinions. If being good made life so hard, I'd just be bad. *If God is out there, He doesn't care. You think I'm poor white trash? Fine. That's what I'll be. But I'm going to have a good time with it.*

Only I wasn't. I wasn't having a good time with it. I was destroyed. Navigating through high school is hard enough with puberty, hormones, insecurity, trying to figure out where you belong and wondering why you don't. But add in poverty, the secret of molestation, an alcoholic, absent dad, and a mother struggling desperately to have hope and strength for her family, and I was just over it. The playful little girl from the middle of the clothes rack slowly faded away. I wasn't good enough. We weren't good enough for a good life. I didn't even want to try. Life was just too disappointing. Even God wanted nothing to do with us. At least that's how I felt.

I couldn't see that it was my decisions that were separating me from Him. He was there. He was *always* there. I was never hidden from Him. He saw me. I just couldn't see Him. All I could see were the looks on the faces of *people*. Stares, glares, sighs, and shaking heads began fogging up my vision when I was just a child. I didn't know anything else. Even then, God had a plan for me. In all the years that I did what I could to destroy myself, He was there keeping me from succeeding. What I didn't know was that He heard every single word of every prayer my mama spoke. I loved her so much, even when I hated her.

I'll never forget one Friday night when I was a freshman. One of the popular girls threw a party. I knew the crowd there would have lots of alcohol, pills, and weed. Despite the hesitation in my gut, I was determined to go. Really, only because I was invited. I was the class clown after all. So my need for acceptance drowned out that still, quiet voice.

I honestly don't even know why. Every time I was around this crowd, I felt out of place. But a lot of the party people were from the wrong side of town too, so if I had a chance at not being looked down on by others, it should be with them, right? I told my mom it was going to be a party of girls and a mom would be there. This mom even told my mom that she'd be home. (She wasn't like a regular mom; she was a cool mom.)

My mom said it was fine because I was so insistent that it would ruin my life if she didn't let me go. But she didn't have a good feeling about it. Nobody did. Even my older sister tried to talk me out of going. She is four years older than me, and even though her friends adored me because I made them laugh, she was pretty annoyed with me 90 percent of the time. She even offered to let me go out with her that night, which *almost* got me. But I wanted friends. I wanted to be accepted by my peers. So I ignored every opportunity I had to make the right choice and went anyway.

As people began showing up to the party, I started to feel more and more uncomfortable. So to loosen up, I started drinking. When my buzz kicked in, better judgment stepped out. I plopped down in the middle of a circle I felt totally uncomfortable in, and I let a boy shotgun some weed into my mouth.

Right about that time, my friend throwing the party came running up to tell me my mom had called several times and left a message that she was coming to get me. I choked on my weed smoke and ran upstairs to listen to this death message. Sure enough. She was coming, and she sounded *ticked*. So, naturally, my mind began to develop all the many excuses I could use to make myself appear innocent. I threw on my pajamas and brushed my teeth—ya know, so she'd think I had been asleep the whole time. I said a few prayers to the same God whom I felt had been ignoring me, because this time my life was at stake.

The doorbell rang. Aggressively. I don't know how my mama made that sweet ding sound so terrifying, but she did. Maybe because it was followed by the pounding of her fist on the door. I tried to open the door and pretend like I was asleep and she had woken me up. I was like, "Mom, you woke me up," and as she hauled me out of that house by my arm, I went into full-blown denial mode. Deny, deny, deny. "I didn't know it was gonna be a party like this, so I went to bed!" I yelled as she yanked me through the front yard.

Now just to paint the picture, I need y'all to know this was a full-blown rager. There were probably sixty teenagers bumping music, smoking, and drinking in the house, in the yard, by the pool. And I'm over here trying to pretend like I was the innocent one, locked in a room asleep. Despite my award-winning performance, Mama wasn't buying it. We got to the middle of the yard, and one of my sister's ex-boyfriends got out of his car holding a case of Coors Light. He obviously didn't notice that my mother was manhandling me out of there, because he looked right at me and said, "Carolanne! Where are you going?" My eyes got *huge*, and I shook my head, shushing him like, *No no no, stop talking.* He then realized who was with me and put his head down, speedwalking to the front door. My mom yelled, "Yeah, Chris, I see you! You have no business here with all these fifteen-year-olds. I suggest y'all get outta here before I call the cops!"

Aggghhh. . .the mortification. I was humiliated. I'd never be invited anywhere ever again because of my psychotic mother who loved me too much. She smacked me half the way home, but truthfully I was so wasted I couldn't even feel it. I think that may have made her madder. Ahhh, good times.

I'm telling you there really is power in a praying mother. My mom said to me that night, "As long as you got a mama that's talking to God, and God's talking to me, you ain't gettin' away with anything."

Looking back at it now, my mom and I laugh

hysterically at how all of that went down. As a teenage girl, I spent so much time thinking I wanted what everyone else had. I wanted the mansion and the money, the clothes, and the freedom to do whatever I wanted. Truth was I had all I needed, I just couldn't see it. I had love in my life. I had a mother who gave a crap. She cared more about my safety than she did about my popularity. She loved me. Though I didn't see it at the time. All I could see was everything I *didn't* have. I completely missed that what I did have was what mattered most. God didn't give us what we wanted; He gave us what we needed. We didn't have abundance, but we had *enough*. What I thought I needed in order to be happy was everything God knew would really destroy me. I made choices over and over again to try to hide from Him, but He just wouldn't let me go. He was never ignoring us. He saw me, and He tried to guide me. But it was my choice to ignore that still, small voice. That night He used my mother's intuition to keep me from only God knows what. I was heading in the wrong direction. I don't want to know what I would have woken up regretting the next day had my mom not listened to her gut.

We can pray all day, but we also need to listen. My mom prayed for my safety, so when God gave her the nudge to protect me, she had to listen.

Sometimes when we feel like we're battling through life's struggles alone, it's because we can't see past the demons blurring our vision. We know what we want, but we can't figure out what it is we are supposed to be learning from the wilderness we find ourselves in. That's where we become who we are in Him. In the wilderness. That's where all the lessons are learned. I wouldn't be who I am right now if I'd received everything I wanted. I was lost because of my own reactions to my circumstances, which led to bad decisions. But when I thought I was in hiding, God was fighting. Fighting for me. Building my character and developing new ways to try to get me back on the path to the plan He had for me. That's why it's so important that we die to ourselves—so we can look, listen, and learn. We shorten the learning curve a bit when we aren't clouded by our own selves.

If you're lost right now, remember that Jesus is *after* you. Don't get mad at me. I didn't say it; He did. As a matter of fact, He legiterally came here and died for the *lost*. He has our backs. Read the Word, y'all. He set people straight when they started getting an attitude about His never-ending pursuit of the wild ones. I truly think a bit of my sarcasm and wit takes after my Savior.

In Luke 15:1–4 when the tax collectors and sinners

gathered to listen to Jesus, the Pharisees muttered, "This man welcomes sinners and eats with them." And I absolutely love that Jesus turned to them without hesitation and said, "Suppose one of you has a hundred sheep and loses one of them. Doesn't he leave the ninety-nine in the open country and go after the lost sheep until he finds it?" *Booooom*. He basically said, "Um, 'scuse Me, Judgy McJudgersons, wouldn't *you* leave the group to find the one who is lost and alone? I mean, I'm just sayin'." I love it. Jesus then pressed them further, asking if they wouldn't rejoice over finding that lost sheep and celebrate with their neighbors. So not only are you supposed to seek those who are lost, ya Pharisee know-it-alls, but you're supposed to *celebrate* when they are found. Listen to what Jesus says here in verse 7: "I tell you that in the same way there will be more rejoicing in heaven over one sinner who repents than over ninety-nine righteous persons who do not need to repent." Say whaaaaat? Can you just imagine the looks on their faces when Jesus put them in their places?

Do you get it? He *will not* let you go. You are the reason for His bloodshed. He wears the holes in His body for you. Don't you see how much He loves you?

I love how Jesus refers to the ninety-nine as being left in the open country where they can easily be found. They are out in plain sight, and they have each other. They aren't hidden; *you are*. It's you He seeks. He has no need to worry about the others, because they already have Him. He wants those who have lost their way. He wants to bring you back to safety, and He wants to throw you a party when you come back home. He's more interested in the humble and meek than the perfect and fake. It's those who have been lost who end up being used as His disciples. Why do you think that is? The lost who have been found carry a light for those who still desperately need guidance.

Luke 15 tells the parable of the lost son. One son takes his inheritance, leaves his father, squanders all his money, realizes his mistakes, and finds his way back home. His father embraces him with open arms, forgiving him and celebrating his return. The other son, who always stood by his father's side, becomes angry and confused. Why does his brother get a celebration like this, and he never did even though he did everything he was supposed to? "My son," the father said, "you are always with me, and everything I have is yours. But we had to celebrate and be glad, because this brother of yours was dead and is alive again; he was lost and is found" (15:31–32).

A selfless, softened heart is required to be like Jesus. There's no place for petty jealousy, judgment, criticism, and condescension if you want to be an effective Christian. We need more disciples trying hard to be more like Jesus and leaving the judgment to God. I can't find any scriptures where Jesus brought a sinner to salvation by using arrogance, threats, and a bad attitude. He didn't step on people; He lifted them higher. He showed them they could walk right beside Him. It was always His love that drew people in. He didn't remind people of all their wrongs and mistakes. Instead, He revealed to them all they could be. He gave them a taste of truth. His peace, joy, and understanding are what He left behind for us to continue passing on to others.

So stop hiding, sisters. God has had His eye on you all along. You may have thought you had the perfect hiding spot, but you'll never be out of His reach—just as my mother never took her eyes off me at the store.

One day I was thinking of all the ways I had tried to run from God, so I wrote a poem. I hope it resonates with you as much as it does with me.

Addicted Amen

I'm drunk, stoned, and stuffed.
It's not enough.
It's not enough.
And it never will be.
There will never be enough to satisfy me.

Because the problem is, I'm not hungry.
My soul is thirsty.
I've had the realization
That my spirit suffers from dehydration.
Thirsty for love.
Thirsty for peace.
My flesh won't set me free.
I need You, Lord.
I'm starving.
There's only regret after the party.
The hole in my heart just gets bigger.
Even when he says I'm sorry.
I shouldn't be so careless with my body.
I didn't realize I was worthy.
I cry myself to sleep.
The absence of her presence cuts so deep.
What can I take to escape the grief?
It's not enough.
Take it. Take this from me.
I'm so sorry.
I know You love me.
I believe it's not just a story.
I'll give You the glory.
Restore me.
Make me new.
Let me see myself from Your point of view.
Fill me with Your Word.

The way, the life, the truth.
I'm addicted to You, Lord.
Take my chains. Give me fruit.
I'm sober.
I'm satisfied.
I'm full.
I'm running to You, Lord.
I can't believe I'm running.
It used to be a *nur*.
But now I'm chasing after something.
Something I can see.
Something I can feel.
You brought my pain up to the surface.
I had to deal so I could heal.
Now it has a purpose.
Life is good.
Despite the struggles.
I can smile in the face of trouble.
I got my laughter back.
She laughs.
I'm without fear when I'm attacked.
I keep on moving.
Forward motion.
You have my full devotion.
It doesn't matter where I've been.
Value isn't found in the opinions of men.
My worth left marks within your skin.

You won't let me stay hidden.
It's Your love, Lord.
I'm addicted, amen.

I hope you know without a doubt there's not a day in your life that the Father isn't pursuing your love. He will seek you forever, no matter how hard you hide.

CHAPTER 6

DEATH TO FLESH

*"I have been crucified with Christ and I no longer
live, but Christ lives in me. The life I now live
in the body, I live by faith in the Son of God,
who loved me and gave himself for me."*
GALATIANS 2:20

"Death to flesh" sounds like a zombie movie. It's one of those phrases I had heard in church when I was a teenager and just rolled my eyes, so annoyed at how dramatic Christians are. Told y'all, just because Mama got us in church doesn't mean I always embraced it. Southern Baptist preacher waving his Bible, red faced, spitting, and dripping with sweat: "You've. Got. To. Die. To. Your. Self. Can I get an amen, ahhh. Not *today*, Devil!" And all the sweet ladies in church would clap, raise their hands, and shout, "Yas, Lord, yaaasss!" while simultaneously shooting daggers over at the kids in the youth group section for passing notes during the sermon. I swear my mama had X-ray vision. I'd look up and see that southern mama stare-down, and I'd slowly back my hand away from my friend's lap—no sudden movements—and hide the note in my palm.

I think my annoyance with church when I was younger stemmed from the new rules we were expected to follow. We had to get dressed up and spend an entire Sunday at this place *and* be on our best behavior. I got my fair share of pinches on the inside of my arm, because as y'all know, I am a little bit talkative. I also had a habit of falling asleep on my mama's shoulder, only to be rudely awakened when she felt my slobber start dripping down her forearm. But I sure did love seeing my friends at Sunday school, feasting on the lunch cooked by the church ladies, and playing Sunday night parking lot football with the older boys and dads while my mama had choir practice. Yep, eight-year-old little tomboy me in the midst of grown men scoring all the touchdowns. They called me "greased lightning." Okay, y'all are getting me way off topic here. Focus, CA, *focus.*

My point is, I didn't understand this concept of "dying to self." The kind of cool, kind of weird thing is, the day I gave my life over to God, I had this lightbulb moment where "dying to self" finally made complete and total sense. Actually, a lot of things started to make sense. I later learned this is called receiving the gifts of the Holy Spirit. I know it sounds a little nutso, but when I researched what those gifts were, I was like, "Ohhh, okay, so this is why so many things are making sense and lining up now." When God said to me, *"Give it up,"* this is what He meant. Giving up my life, giving up control, giving up worry and fear, giving up anger and all the negative things my soul clings to. You gotta let it all die so that God can open your eyes to all the beautiful things the world has been hiding from you. Letting go of pride in the moment is a tough thing to do when giving yourself over. You have to be willing to be humbled and ready to accept that you don't always know what you're doing. Have you ever tried to help someone who just wasn't ready to receive it? They ask for advice, but nothing changes because they change nothing. Some people refer to these individuals as ask-holes. LOL. That was sooo not a curse word, sheesh! Well, if we're being honest, we've all been one of these a time or two—and will be one again, I'm sure. Our old tendencies and thought processes will always creep back in, so we just need to keep working at it and doing our best.

I think there is another reason some people have to be completely brokenhearted before they are willing to let their walls come down: they gotta be stripped of all their pride. For me it was seeing someone I loved more than myself suffering in a way that I could do nothing about. It made me realize that so many of the stupid things I worry about each day are insignificant. Ya know? Like why do we care so much about what people think of us? Why do we hide who we are? Why do we put on fake, filtered faces to please people who have no real importance to the purpose of our existence? I mean, we know on some level that no matter what we do, there will never be a time when everyone likes us. So if we're gonna be disliked either way, why not at least feel the freedom, peace, and joy of being who we are and doing what we love? Make that silly video, belt it out at open mic night, type out the title of that book you've always wanted to write, train for that marathon, pursue the career you dream about.

The first time I let myself be completely real, I nearly choked to death on my own spit while pushing it a little too good, all while my one-year-old screamed like a dying cat over an iPad game. And I was terrified to show it to the world. But I made the decision to let others see something real, goofy, lighthearted, and fun, because life is too short not to laugh. Dying to myself resulted in dying to the weight of what others may think of me. God took over, and He gave me the freedom to be me—even when I'm acting a fool.

This whole "death to self" thing isn't just a one-time deal, though. I have to be humbled over and over again, and that's okay. I always know when I've started trying to take back control. It's usually when life begins to feel overwhelming and stressful. Sometimes I get ahead of myself and try to force things to happen. I stop trusting God's timing, because He's taking too long. Every time I try to make stuff happen, I get myself in a position where I've got too many plates to carry. Then I start dropping them and feeling like a failure, questioning myself and everything He promised me. Meanwhile, I'm pretty sure God is just rolling His eyes like, *My goodness, child, when are you gonna learn that I've got you?*

We have a hard time getting over ourselves, don't we? I mean, how many times have you just waited on someone to stop talking so you could reply? How many times have you completely missed out on what God was teaching you in a moment because you were too busy arguing before He was even finished? (Some of y'all might be doing that reading this book right now.) I'm stubborn. I can be set in my ways. I'm also defensive. But when you live life on the defense, nobody can help you. They don't get you or your life, and they don't understand your situation; so no matter how great their point is, you are just going to twist and manipulate it until it means what you want it to.

I fight with the Holy Spirit all the time. One time, I convinced myself that it was God's plan for me to be on Jen Hatmaker's podcast. She's a well-known author and speaker in the realm I know I've been called to be in. So when I heard she was coming to my teeny tiny town to speak and that there were meet-and-greet tickets, I jumped all over it like, *Praise the Lord, He has opened up a door for me to make a great connection and we are gonna be best friends and she is gonna know exactly who I am and I'm gonna be on her podcast. Woot, woot!* I had a slight hesitation, though, so obviously I rebuked it quickly. *Not today, Devil!* I bought the more expensive ticket, got there, stood in line, and psyched myself up to say hi. I walked up sweaty and awkward to stumble through saying, "I'm not sure if you recognize my name, but I'm CA Miljavac." I got a slightly awkward but polite smile, and she was so sweet, but she had no idea who I was. Y'all, I had an actual Ron Burgundy "I don't know if you know who I am, but I'm kind of a big deal" moment. I was like, *Wait, that's not how that was supposed to go down.* So I went back in for the second meet-and-greet and just made it doubly awkward. It was a total flop, and once again I was reminded that when my gut tells me I'm wrong but my flesh gets all excited, I need to step back and wait.

I knew I needed to chill out, but I have a habit of ignoring God when He says, *"Be still."* Good news is, I'm no stranger to embarrassing myself, so now I just laugh. But I'm working on taming my emotions, even the good ones. My emotions are a part of my flesh I have to work on letting die. I get excited about what God's doing in my life, but excitement can be as distracting as any other emotion. It's good that I know God has good plans for me, but I still need to let Him work them out in His timing. Always learning lessons and accumulating great stories in the process. I just need to relax and be patient. Pray before I "slay."

You gotta know who you truly are—in your spirit. You have to get away from your flesh in order to see it. Your flesh will get all up in your way, because it usually can't see past how you feel. . .and how you feel is easily influenced by other people.

You know why Jesus bothered people so much? He knew who He was. He knew who He belonged to. Nobody could tell Him any different. So not only do we have this guy walking around spittin' hard-to-hear convicting truths. . .but now He is all confident and self-assured too? And *nice*? That doesn't sit well with people who are lost. With people who have convinced themselves that life is as it should be, and that means hardship and misery. People who are unwilling to admit they are making bad decisions. They get nervous when the truth begins to threaten the way of life they've become addicted to. Pleasures of the flesh always seem right at the time.

"Now this Jesus guy is gonna come over here and make me feel bad about it? Who does He think He is?"

"Well, He says He's the Son of God."

"Oh heeeck no. Let's keep up with Him, though, just to see what else He says."

We are so funny like that. Social media, for example. How many people do you see trollin' pages so hard, but they *stay*. We get mad at 'em, but the truth is they stay because some piece of them wants to see it. Wants to hear it. Their spirit feels a stirring, and their flesh is ticked about it. Why? Because our flesh is of the world. Who rules the world? I'll wait. . .

You got it. Satan.

So when Satan sees someone stirring up your spirit, what starts to happen? You begin to feel conflicted. Sometimes angry and defensive. I get so mad when Jesus calls me out. We don't want our way of life threatened. Even if we aren't particularly happy, we get very rooted in our ways. But the truth is, a lot of the things we're holding on to are the things making us unhappy. We don't wanna hear that. I don't want to hear that I don't need to eat a bag of Cheetos late at night with a 20 ounce Coke. I love Cheetos. I love the fake cheese crumbs piled up at the bottom of the bag. I love scraping my finger through 'em and licking it off. (Don't even act like you're grossed out by that. You know you do it too!) But I can't do that all the time and feel good. I don't want to hear that it would be better for me to go to bed early instead of staying up late for my "mommy" me-time. But the truth is, if I feel like an unproductive zombie each day relying on coffee to function, it's my fault. I could go to bed early and then wake up earlier for some healthier me-time with a half hour of good reading, prayer, a good breakfast, and a better day.

Your spirit, your gut, your instinct will lead you in a direction that's best for you and best for others in the long run. It's called *discernment*—when you're faced with a decision and you want to make a certain choice, but something keeps telling you to go a different path. Let me give you an example. I was never an everyday smoker in my younger years. I'd smoke socially, when I was drinking, or just as a rebellious way to give the finger to the overbearing, hyperjudgy people at the Church of Christ college where I played softball. (I was a little bit of a sassy-frass.) But I was never addicted to cigarettes. So the summer I found out I was pregnant, it was easy for me to put them away. Two kids later, during a rare girls' night out, a friend asked if I wanted a cigarette. And I did want one. For no other reason than just to do it. I just wanted to let loose. But even as I said, "Yes!" the word "No" was flashing through my mind. Why? If I wanted it and didn't think it was that big of a deal, why was everything in me saying, *You shouldn't be smoking this*? I had the discernment even then; I just didn't listen.

There's no place in your soul for self-destruction, because your Creator loves you too much. That's when conviction sets in. I think a lot of people might avoid completely giving themselves over to God because they don't want to be convicted. You gotta be humbled and broken down, willing to admit your way isn't better, before He can take you higher.

———

"Truly, truly, I say to you, unless a grain of wheat falls into the earth and dies, it remains alone; but if it dies, it bears much fruit."
JOHN 12:24 ESV

God sure does work in mysterious ways, doesn't He? You gotta die to the world if you want to live in the truth. I wasn't willing to experience life to the fullest until my niece lost hers. I just don't care anymore what the world wants, what I want, or what other people want. I just want what God wants. I won't be here forever. I don't want to leave this earth with nothing good to be remembered by. I don't want to live selfishly; I want to deposit a tiny piece of the me Christ created in the hearts of as many people as I can I want to do that for Ansley. I want to do that for my children. I don't want to live a life less than what God intended.

Y'all know, despite the current state of the world and all the negative current events, you can still have joy. You can still have peace. You can seriously do *anything* you want to do—with God's help. Your view of life is so much clearer without the world throwing shade on your vision. Satan makes you feel like it's over for you. He wants you to think you've dug yourself in too deep and there's no way out. He is a *liar face*. The Holy Spirit can guide you out of the deepest, darkest ditch your life has ever known. Jesus is the way, the truth, and the life. And if you hand yourself over to Him, He will prove it. I'm telling you He will blow your mind. Like John 12:24 says, if you die you will bear *so much fruit*. Like the good kind of fruit without pesticides and all that other junk. Organic fruit, y'all. Juicy fruit. The kind of fruit everybody wants to taste because it's just so sweet and life-changing. This ain't no regular old fruit. It's so much tastier than that fruit-like poison the world is serving. Ya get what I'm sayin'?

Nothing in this world tastes as good as the fruit of freedom. That's what you get when you let your flesh go. You get to be happy. You get to forgive and move on. You can look forward to what tomorrow brings instead of spewing worry and what-ifs all over your life and everyone around you. Freedom will help you feel the fear and do it anyway. It opens doors *no one* can shut. It lets you loose out in the world. You won't die alone, because you will have planted seeds everywhere you went. Seeds of hope, kindness, wisdom, laughter, and joy.

You will never live completely sheltered from evil, but trust me when I say you have armor. Shed your skin and strap on your shield. The armor of God doesn't just protect you; it helps you protect others. Your defense is found in praise, prayer, and the Word of God. It's in the truth. Love cannot be conquered, and there is power in the tongue. So shout God's praises, speak the truth, share your story, say your prayers. Speak it, sisters! Let 'em know. Let the enemy know who you belong to. Let the world know the work that has been accomplished inside your heart. God takes your heart of stone and turns it to flesh. His Spirit softens you up to your troubles. You *feel* it, don't you? Don't you feel the difference?

I used to be so stubborn that I'd argue with anyone who tried to tell me how much better their life was with Jesus than what I had without Him. I would get so annoyed, because I did believe in Jesus, but I was thinking, *Y'all just assume I don't because you think I'm beneath you.* I'd think they were just judging me. I'd think, *I'm plenty happy, and you don't know what you're talking about.* I was so blind. What people who don't "get it" can't understand is this *feeling* inside; it can't even be described.

You can see it in people you know. It's a lightness. They walk without the weight of chains. They stand tall and stand out. They have plenty of troubles but don't let the stress get to them. They can smile when they shouldn't. They have joy in times of struggle. You just want to be around them. They aren't sucking the light out of the room with their negativity like so many others whose hearts are stubborn and hard.

Sister, are you running from the responsibility of your purpose? Are you afraid you can't sustain what it takes to live out your calling? I have been scared so many times, worried that I couldn't keep the gifts God gave me at the level at which He set the bar. It's hard to accept that we are exceptional. That He makes us capable. Does it scare you a bit to think that little ol' you could leave a mark? Ya know, what people think is a "hard life" is often much easier than living at the level you could be—being healthy, happy, and at peace inevitably requires the removal of things that make us comfortable. You might need to cut out late-night TV so you can get up earlier for some "me-time." You might need to replace Coke with water (everything is Coke where I come from. We ask, "What kind of Coke do you want?"). It's easy going through the same motions every day, never challenging yourself to change. But living at a higher level means changing up your daily routine. Getting up and going to a job you hate might not be enjoyable, but it's easy to do. Being in a relationship that makes you miserable might be easier than getting out of the relationship, even if it's better for you. It takes no effort, no change, no risk, no sacrifice to live a mediocre life. It's an action step of faith to embrace the challenge to live out your full potential. *Sista, preach!*

Don't get mad at me. That's your flesh feeling called out a bit. Listen, I'm feeding y'all off my own plate here. There's not a thing I'm saying that I don't need to hear and be reminded of myself. But come on, y'all! You know there's a tug on your heart for some gift or vision you've held yourself back from. You fear it might not be true. The enemy challenges you with doubts of your ability. Who do you think you are to think you could teach, speak life, perform surgery, save a life, write meaningful poetry? There's a reason your passions keep coming back to you. You won't keep having visions or desires to do things that aren't a part of who you are. Sometimes we just have it all jumbled up.

I wanted to be on *Saturday Night Live* when I was young. I also wanted to be an Olympic athlete, a TV reporter, a comedy actress, and Jessica Rabbit. My visions weren't crystal clear, but I can see how my destiny has lined up with all the things my heart kept being drawn to. It took me thirty years, though, to listen to my spirit. But guess what had to happen first? Death to self. That day in my car when God told me I'd speak, instead of doing what I wanted to do and scoffing it off as a crazy idea that would never happen, I had to say yes. Why? Because I no longer belonged to me. I died to my ways and pledged my faith. If God tells me I can, I can. Period.

It's your flesh that lies to you. The enemy loves to use your own thoughts and the opinions of others to keep you from pursuing your purpose. I let the opinion of someone I respected keep me from trying out for the Olympic softball team. I laughed when my speech teacher gave me a 100 and told me I needed to pursue a speaking career. I blew off my humor as useless. "Who do you think you are? You can't do it. You aren't good enough. There's no point in trying.

Don't forget where you came from. You're not that funny. You don't have the money. That was just a fluke. You don't have it in you. You'll give up."

Those doubts always stemmed from the enemy. Always. You know why? Why does he care so much? What is gonna happen if people start stepping into their passion? What is gonna happen if we get a taste of what God can do with us?

We'd begin to understand that there's nothing the enemy can give us that God can't use *for* us. When he put us through hell, we'd take fuel from the fire and blow it up in his face! Like a Chuck Norris missionary messenger ninja of God. (Okay, that got a little out of hand. My Southern Baptist background slipped out—talking passionate nonsense, hopping up and down, all fired up for the Lord. I love it. I mean it, though.) You can't be stopped when you know who you are. So here are a few steps to help understand yourself better.

1. *Have a quiet time.* Take five to ten minutes minimum each day to sit in silence, distraction free. No phone, no music, no TV, no nothing. Moms, I know you're thinking, *What is this silence you speak of?* Maybe it's early morning before everyone wakes up. Maybe it's late at night after they go to

sleep. Maybe it's a sprint to sit alone in your car when your spouse gets home. Make it happen. No excuses.

2. *Read.* There's no shortage of inspiring, thought-provoking, encouraging books out there. A few of my favorites are *Fervent* by Priscilla Shirer, *Uninvited* by Lysa TerKeurst, and *Battlefield of the Mind* by Joyce Meyer. Reading gets your wheels turning. It helps bring memories and feelings to the surface.

3. *Journal.* Write down any thoughts that come to you during your quiet or reading time. Journal each day how you're feeling, and reflect on other times in your life when you felt that way. Put the thoughts you usually push to the back of your mind on paper. Or start a blog. Bloggers will tell you that the more you say about your day, the better you feel, for real.

4. *Get to know yourself.* When you meet someone new, you ask them plenty of questions to get to know them better. So go ahead and introduce yourself. . .to yourself! Turn those questions on yourself. Don't just answer, but dig deeper so you understand where your answers come from. What are my habits, favorites, triggers, tendencies, and *why, why, why*?

Always ask why until there's nothing left to dig up.

5. *Get into the Word.* Learn what God says about you. Really dwell on exactly what was sacrificed for you and why. What did Jesus see in you? If you don't know where to start, it's easy to pick something you struggle to believe about yourself and just search that keyword in scripture. Then open up your Bible to that scripture and read it over and over with your mind open to the Lord's guidance.

Self-reflection is a great way to really get to know your character, morals, and values. If you will let God mold you, He will use you to send a message with the example of your life. People will see something in you that they want to have in their own lives. You'll get your fair share of kickback from all the people out there parked in their own self-pity—those unable to be happy for anyone. But even they will come around if you stand rooted in the truth. When doubt creeps in, pour the Word into your flesh. Songs, sermons, motivational speeches, books, podcasts, you name it. Anything that fuels you back up.

Death to flesh isn't about losing yourself or changing who you are. It's about blossoming into the best version of you. It's allowing your Christ-filled spirit to lead the way instead of your own mind and desires. It's acquiring discernment, guidance, and wisdom. It's getting over yourself and into your spirit. It's being humble yet confident. Prideless but strong. You are dying to the lusts of humankind to live for the will of God. Dying to sinful ways that end up hurting you and others.

I want to have more of Christ's love in my heart and less of me. How about you? I'm not afraid to admit that the more of me I live by, the worse my life gets. My flesh carries hurt feelings, anger, regret, shame, doubt, confusion, depression, and self-destructive habits. That's what the world has built into me. So I ask Him with genuine sincerity, "Tear down the wall. Break me apart. Brick by brick, destroy this foundation and let's start over. Reveal to me what You've rebuilt in me every time You put me back together. I'm ready. I'm willing. Nothing else matters. Bury my burdens, Lord. I don't want them anymore. Let me live for You and do something meaningful with the time I'm given here in this life. Less me, more You. So much that it overflows onto everyone around me."

You should totally have a Happy Death-to-Self Day party! Here's what you need:

Song: "Bye Bye Bye" by NSYNC. Obvi.

Food: According to John 6, Jesus is the

bread of life, so I'm thinking footlong subs for everyone.

Game: Twister. 'Cause your stubborn butt will probably hold that uncomfortable position as long as possible before giving in and falling. God loves that about you. It's a part of who you are, and you'll need to be stubborn when the world wants to sway your faith.

CHAPTER 7

Control Freak

"Do not worry about your life, what you will eat;
or about your body, what you will wear. For life is
more than food, and the body more than clothes.
Consider the ravens: They do not sow or reap, they
have no storeroom or barn; yet God feeds them.
And how much more valuable you are than birds!"
LUKE 12:22-24

Any of y'all have an issue sitting still? I'm an antsy mess. I've actually contemplated getting "Be still" tattooed on my forearm to remind me to chill out. 'Cause I got issues.

But all of us do, right?

I have found that the more overwhelmed I get, the less productive I am. Which leads to more piled up, and me in bed eating a bag of Cheetos, upset that I've gained twenty—okay, thirty—"stress pounds" because of all the things I haven't done and nobody will help me so it's not even my fault.

Myyy goodness. Makes sense, right?

It's like when you need to clean, you try to stick to an actual list of things to do. But when you were walking toward the dishes, you got real bothered by the trash, but can't take it out because six loads of laundry hiding behind your bedroom door are eating at you, and on your way to deal with that you notice dust particles floating in the air so you go to the Targets for an air purifier and come home with a towel set instead. Then your husband lets you know his mom is stopping by in twenty minutes, and you become a cross between Martha Stewart and Joanna Gaines on speed and sugar. You dust, mop, put matching socks on your kids (because she needs to know you have your life together), clip their nails, organize, fluff pillows and place them over all the Lord-knows-what stains on your stupid microfiber couch that's just so great for kids according to the salesman (who must have no kids), cook some ordoovres (gotta spell it how you say it), and shower with twelve seconds to spare and you even dried your hair. It's all about the mind-set.

Some of you might be laughing because I'm describing you. Don't worry, I won't judge. I have my crap together, so I don't really know what that's like, but it sounds terrible. Bless your hearts.

Y'all just need to learn to identify and deny when the enemy gets in those thoughts. Ya know, rebuke him. The idea of telling him *no* out loud used to make me laugh. I'd imagine an old lady walking around her kitchen like, "Not *taday*, Satan!" Then I saw the movie *War Room* and just fell in love with Miss Clara. She was the embodiment of everything I imagined when it came to a faithful Christian. She is #goals. Brutal honesty delivered with wisdom in a loving, humorous way. A courageous commitment to loving others (even those who already know God) straight back to Jesus. I'm pretty good at the whole "rebuking the devil" thing now. A little too good. Sometimes I'm casting out thoughts all day long.

Crying in my car like, "My baby girl is starting preschool next year and I'm gonna be all alone for the rest of my life. . . . Whyyyyy? It's too soon. I'm not ready. Maybe I should have another. Nooope, that was a thought straight from the devil, but I see ya, Satan, and you know what I'm sayin'—not taday!" The good Lord knows I ain't trying to have a fourth daughter unless it's in His plan. I don't need to be trying to make a baby when my rationale is clouded over with the image of my youngest child bebopping all over my heart on her way into preschool.

Everyone knows you don't drunk dial or make babies on the first day of drop-off.

Or how many of y'all have done this: "I've been growing my hair out for three years, but it's bothering me today so instead of a trim let's just do a pixie. *Neeerp. Phew!* The enemy about got me like Delilah got Samson. Get thee behind me, ya liar face!"

Ahhh, so yeah, sometimes I might rebuke a few too many things, but at least I've got discernment.

Okay, for real now. . .all jokes aside, because those last few paragraphs were entirely sarcasm. I don't actually do *any* of that (winky face). Truth is, when I don't slow down and listen, it's easy for the enemy to influence my decisions using my emotions. It's feeling unsettled. It's overthinking and worrying. Honestly, it just sucks. Sucks the peace right out of you. When you let God have control, He'll make it clear to you when it's time to take authority over the enemy.

Giving up control was absolutely essential to finding peace in my life. It restored joy to my spirit and broke off a ton of chains. When chains are broken, you are set free to live your life to the absolute fullest. People ask me all the time *how* I gave up control, so I'm gonna tell ya the story of the first time I let go and how I continue to let go, as the enemy will always sling more at you to keep you in bondage.

I. Was. Broken.

For starters, I really and truly expected very little of myself. By the time I reached middle school, life had already jaded any hopes and dreams that used to stir up in my spirit. Over time, I developed a hardened heart toward the world, people, and my potential. The enemy started on me early. You know that he *knows* what God could do with you, right? That's why he hates families, and especially children. Children are so innocently full of ambition, dreams, and aspirations. They haven't been jaded just yet to what they may not realize is the voice of God planting potential in their hearts. For many adults, His voice is barely an audible whisper, drowning in the shouts of the enemy's lies. But when I was young, I had that childlike belief that *anything is possible*. So the enemy took chunks out of me at an early age. He used poverty, alcohol, abandonment, abuse, and bullying to build a wall around my spirit and dim the light until it was hardly visible. That tough, thick rhino skin wouldn't let anyone hurt me. But it led to a way of living that was either completely irresponsible or exhaustively stubborn. I had this "I'm on my own, gotta do what I gotta do" attitude, so I'd just tackle way too much head-on with the idea that the only way I'd get through life was if I bulldozed my way through it.

The slow and steady persistence of a flower allows it to sprout through a concrete sidewalk, keeping every one of its petals in place. You don't have to move at the pace of everyone else. Rely on God's timing. When our babies don't listen to us, we put them in time-out. Time to just sit and think about what we told them and why. Time for them to learn from their mistake. Because in the real world you can't spit on people when they take something you want. Because that's gross and unsanitary, and you'll end up dehydrated.

Sometimes we need to be still and listen, so God will make us wait. Then we can learn while we observe from the sidelines. I've watched so many people pass me by. Job advancements, recognition, awards—you name it. Sometimes I would get so frustrated thinking, *Why not me? I worked so hard,* or *I did that first.* But I learned so much in those times. I learned that what I want isn't always what I need. For example, social media. Everyone thinks it's so cool to have a bunch of viral videos and fans. But it's also overwhelming and mentally exhausting. You can begin losing your identity to the opinions of people who don't even know you. God has taught me that I don't always do well with recognition. It challenges the redneck woman in me to come out from time to time. God lets me know when I need a break. So I trust His timing. All I need is Him. If anything begins to threaten that, He removes it. He is in control.

When my feelings and I are in control, I sometimes put the "hot" in "psychotic." Like throwing my husband's Dr Peppers in the front yard to get back at him for clipping his nails in my bed. I mean, who does that? I see you slowly raising your hand, crazy pants. I know I'm not the only wife here who has had those moments. But even the craziest of my emotions are not outside God's power to temper if I give it up to Him.

Have you ever allowed a Facebook status, by some person you haven't seen in twenty-five years, to ruin your whole dang day because you disagreed with them? Think about how silly that is. Did you forget that before the days of social media, there were people out there who didn't view life just like you? It's a miracle to start and finish a day with a good attitude when your joy depends on what's going on around you. Feelings are finicky. Did you know it's possible to feel annoyed, angry, or sad and still maintain joy, peace, and laughter? I'm telling you it is such a good feeling not to be a puppet to your emotions. You'll have a lot less regret.

Giving God control gives you a sense of ease, because no matter what happens or what anybody says or does to you, you completely trust God to do whatever needs to be done with it. Sometimes you might feel like He's not doing anything with it. Maybe you start to get a bit impatient, or you don't like the way things are working out. But from my own experience, I don't find out until later on, in His timing, why things panned out the way they did. I have realized that there's so much I can't see that He sees. There's so much I'll never know that He knows. So we just keep growing slow and steady, until eventually we blossom right through even the hardest of times. With God in control, something good can be worked out from it.

Take Me, for Example

I was thirty years old before I'd finally had it with trying to do things my way. It took someone I loved more than I love myself suffering immensely to humble me enough to wave the white flag. To let Jesus take the wheel, the gearshift, the gas pedal, and steer.

Now, since I am antsy and stubborn as a mule, I obviously try from time to time to backseat drive until I annoy God so much that He throws Himself out of the car and I end up crashing. Then I say sorry and ask if He'd like to drive again, promising to sit still and just enjoy the ride. It's a trust thing. It's tough to adjust after years of broken trust in people. But

He understands, and He won't hold it against you. So you can crash the car over and over and over, and He'll always get back in and get you back on track. Isn't that such sweet relief? Bottom line: if you are consumed with worry, fear, and unrest over your future, you are not letting Him have control. Not really.

So what does it look like to let God steer? In my own life, it was saying yes to opportunities that aligned with the calling He spoke to me. Speaking. I didn't want to do it. I was really scared in the beginning. The first speech I ever gave, I thought I was gonna puke, go blank, or have massive sweat spots on my shirt. But I asked Him for discernment and clarity when opportunities presented themselves. Sometimes an opportunity would seem cool, but He'd give me a feeling that I should say no. Usually to protect me from getting overwhelmed and shutting down. He knows me well. I tend to become depressed when too many people want too much from me.

Discernment is almost impossible to receive when you aren't having daily conversations with the Lord. Conversations, not requests. I mean, just talk to Him. Before you call your mom, talk to your best friend, or ask someone on Facebook, make sure you let Him know what's going on and how you're feeling. The gift of the Spirit will show you the way in due time. When my thoughts are just completely out of control, drowning out clarity, it's usually when I've crept away from essential time with the Lord. It's crucial to give yourself a solid ten to twenty minutes each day of silence, prayer, meditation, and self-reflection. That's your time for building your relationship with the Lord, allowing Him to restore your peace, and getting in touch with your thoughts. If you do this every day, I *promise* you will find yourself better able to make good decisions and handle whatever life throws at you with strength, dignity, and grace. Kinda like that Proverbs 31 lady who has it all together. She is an inspiration, isn't she? Used to just annoy me, but really she's a reflection of what happens when the fruit of the Spirit grows within your soul. I want to be kind, hardworking, courageous, understanding, hard to offend, grateful, and full of laughter. I'm closer to that today than I was three years ago. But let's be clear: we will always be a work in progress, and that's not only okay but what makes us all different and valuable to each other.

―――――――――

On my most broken day, when the still, small voice said, *"Give it up,"* I just threw my hands up and said, "Okay." Nothing super poetic. Just "Okay."

Okay, I'm not gonna fight You anymore.

Okay, I'm not gonna live for myself and what makes me happy anymore.

Okay, I'll sacrifice some things I enjoy if it means my life will serve a purpose.

And this is where things really got tricky for me. We all feel conviction over different things. For me personally, words became very important. I'm thinking it's probably because there's such a strong calling on me to speak. So I just became very aware of the language I was using. Have you ever seen the movie *Liar Liar* with Jim Carrey? His character cannot physically tell a lie. He tries and just can't get it to come out. Cursing started to feel that way to me. It seems like such a small thing, and yet it bothers people so much that I don't curse. (Unless my husband clipping his toenails in my bed brings out the redneck woman in me. But I already apologized.) If I slip up and do curse, I immediately feel regretful. It's just my own personal conviction, but I've noticed people react strangely to it. As if my choice means they can't either, or that I'll think less of them. Of course, that's not true at all. I'm just listening to my own spirit. I honestly have no control over what will convict me personally. I've noticed the more changes I make that aren't popular with the crowd, the fewer friends I have. Living for God goes hand in hand with developing into the absolute best version of yourself, whatever that looks like for you. No doubt this will make others uncomfortable when it looks different from how they live their lives. But it goes both ways. Sometimes other people *will* actually try to make you feel bad if you're not what they consider to be Christian-like. *Do not listen to them.* Live your life as best as you can, and don't worry about what anyone thinks. God is perfectly capable of dealing with you if and when needed. Nobody is perfect. Your pursuit of your best life doesn't mean you think you're better than anybody. And don't let anyone convince you otherwise. It's difficult and it's tricky, but you just stay focused on what He's doing through you, because that's what's most important.

So now, every time I find myself feeling alone and isolated, I have to remind myself to be still and get back to God. I usually sit in my car for quiet time. It's the only place I'm completely alone. . .for a little while. *They* always find me. So in my garage before my kids figure out where I've run off to, I'll sit in silence and imagine all of the things I've been worried about floating above me like balloons. I picture myself letting them go. I see them float farther and farther away from me, and I see God grab the strings attached to them and carry them off. I always feel immediate relief and peace. Let your worries go so you're left only with God. Let your heart be okay with that. Trust and believe that He is enough for you. When He is enough, it's not so hard to cast your cares. Y'all, you'll be okay. You're gonna make it. You *are* making it.

There's not a single season of my life that I didn't get through, because *here I am*. Getting through it. Moving forward. You are getting through whatever it is you are going through *right now*. You will make it, and you will be okay. God has good plans for you, if you will stay rooted through the worst of seasons.

———————

When I was in junior college playing softball, there was a time when I had almost nothing to my name. I got a scholarship, but I didn't have money to stay in the apartments on campus. I had a clunker car, but no money for gas to travel thirty minutes home and back for class and practice. My mom had no money to give me. Maybe a twenty-dollar bill here and there. So I lived out of my car. Everything I owned I kept in the trunk of my car that I parked at the apartments where my softball team lived on campus. I slept on a futon in the living room of my best friend/catcher. The first week of school, my car quit on me. So everywhere I went, I either walked or caught a ride with my teammates. The days when I had no classes with them, I'd have to carry in my arms all the books for every class I had that day and just sprint from building to building to make it to each class. At the time, I was so tired of struggling with things it seemed no one else had to deal with. I was the only one with no car, no food, no money, no space of my own.

I always felt like such a burden on everyone, and I hated always needing help. I had no pride. There was none to be had. I was a walking charity case, and it made me feel worthless. There were days I sat down at the ball field alone, just crying and asking whatever it was that my mama said existed in the sky why I always had to have it so much harder than everyone else. *Why me? Why us? Why our family?* I was trying so hard to do the right thing. To get a college degree and maybe even earn a four-year scholarship at a university if I worked hard enough at this two-year degree. I gave every softball practice everything I had. I showed up to class a sweaty mess carrying all my books because I couldn't afford a backpack. I was so tired of the simple things for everyone else being *so hard* for me. I'd cry and curse and feel sorry for myself for a little while, and then I'd take a deep breath and get back to it.

One day it dawned on me how lucky I was to always have really, *really* good friends around me, who truly didn't mind taking me in, feeding me, and being my friend. One thing I did have was an ability to make people laugh, and that led to some amazing friendships with people who wanted me around. I was so focused on how hard life was and so wrapped up in my feelings that I didn't think to be grateful for the people God had placed in my life to help get me through these hard times that ultimately were crafting all kinds of character in me. These wonderful friends took me in and shared their living space with me. We actually thought it was pretty fun hiding all my stuff from the RA when she did room checks, like my friends were harboring a fugitive or something. They let me eat with them. They even took me home with them sometimes on long weekends to stay with their families, even though I had no money. On the field I was a leader; off the field I was humbled. I needed this softball team so badly. I needed these girls in my life. I needed this sport and my coach. I wanted to control everything; but when you have nothing, there's not really anything to control. You are just dependent on others.

This was the first time in my life that I began feeling a stirring in my spirit. I was eighteen and feeling very alone at times. My coach believed in me so much, and I really wanted to make him proud...and I started thinking about my future. I had alienated myself, because a baseball player had said he loved me, and so I devoted all my free time to him. Of course, he broke up with me, like eight different times, and then I was left all alone. I hated being alone, but it was only then that I felt a connection with what I could only assume was God.

I told y'all I got saved when I was eight years old, but I went through many years of not really understanding what a relationship with God was like. I knew the rules of religion, but nothing of an actual connection. I just had this feeling that I could be better. But I didn't know how. At the time all I knew of being good for God was following a bunch of rules. So in college I stopped cussing, drinking, even thinking of boys—ya know, all the fun things—and started focusing on softball, school, and learning more about God. It was something I tried to force. It became clear to me later, when Ansley got sick, that God really was always after me; I just let the world get in my way.

I reluctantly went to weekly meetings on campus for a Bible study, or something like a Bible study. I never felt more out of place my whole life. Attending the meetings was really just an attempt to earn brownie points from God, I think. I didn't know then that's not how it works. But He knew my heart; and although I was going about it all wrong, He saw me trying. I prayed every single night. I prayed for everyone I loved. I thanked God for what I did have, and I prayed for the things I felt I really needed—including a car. I really needed a car. I had no idea how it would happen, but I just threw it out there each night, asking that I'd somehow be able to get one even if it was a crap wagon. I just needed something. This went on for several months, and I stayed strong and resisted temptations to party, which caused some of my friendships to suffer. I didn't really know what I was doing, and deep down I knew I was going about this whole relationship with God thing wrong, but still I was learning. He knew I was learning, and He knew I'd figure it out. I'd dip my toes in and then jump back out. It wasn't time for the encounter I was destined to have.

God isn't after picture-perfect good behavior. He's after your heart. He wants you to *want* to know Him. And He'll give you space to figure it all out. He's got you. His plans for you are good, and that means the real you. Wherever you are, whatever season you're in, He knows who you're gonna become, so He allows you to make the mistakes that will help you get there.

———

One day my teammates and I were at practice, and I was in line waiting to bat. My mom had stopped by that day, which was odd (she was always working). But she said she was passing through, so she wanted to see me. All of a sudden this beautiful, bright, brand-new, canary-yellow Chevrolet Cavalier came driving down the gravel road up to the field. None of us were sure who it could be. Nobody recognized the car. When the door opened, my papa stepped out. Papa Bob worked at Carl Cannon Chevrolet for so long, he was always driving different cars. I just thought, *Oh, how nice, my papa came to see me too.* I waved at him, feeling so happy he was there, and turned around to go bat. The entire team was just staring at me, grinning. My head coach was looking like he was gonna cry. My assistant coach was looking like she was gonna explode. My heart started to flutter, and my eyes started to water, and I was just thinking, *What? What is happening?*

Nobody said anything. I turned and looked at my mom, who was now crying. I looked at my papa, and I just said, "Is that for me? No, that's not for me, is it? Is that for me?"

The whole team rushed to me, and everyone was so excited and jumping around and my coach said, "That's for you, Sunshine. Go take it for a spin." He always called me Sunshine. He said I was full of light. He was one of the first people in my life to see that in me, even though I was so blind to it. I ran over to my mom and my papa and just cried and cried. It was the first time in my life that I felt special. It was the first time I owned something nice and new. Something of my own. Papa drove that car straight off the lot to the ball field. I had been praying for a clunker for months.

My family told me after a ton of discussion, my papa felt like, since I was his only grandchild still in college, earning a scholarship and trying to get more out of life than what my circumstances had given me, I deserved the car. He worked it out with my mom and got it for me. I had *no idea* it was even possible. But y'all, this is the first time that I realized just how big God really is. I went from sitting alone at the field asking God why I had to have it so much harder than everyone else, to having the nicest, shiniest, brightest car in the parking lot. But it wasn't about the car. It was what the car represented. This car became a symbol of possibility. It was a reminder that I'm not alone, that I'm not destined for hardship, and that if I did my best to put God first, I'd have what I needed—and if it be His will, *more* than what I needed.

This is a materialistic thing, and I'm sure some of you are thinking, *What about really serious prayers that aren't being answered?* I hear you. I'd have swapped not being molested, poverty, bullying, and an alcoholic father for that car any day. But I trust in God, and all these years later, looking back I know that this was exactly what my heart and soul needed at the time to show me I had a better life ahead if I kept the faith. This is *my* story, and everyone's story is different. *He* knew what was in store for me, and I truly believe this was an answered prayer. But I had to give Him control of the situation. I had to quit pressing it and stressing it, and finally just make the best of my situation trusting that I would be okay. It wasn't until I had a grateful heart for what I had that I was blessed with more.

If I had decided to be angry and rebel, because what's the point of even trying anymore, I wouldn't have ended up getting that car. I would have ended up in trouble, my scholarship lost, back at home doing nothing with my life with a future looking dim. But if you'll just *be still* and *know*, not doubt or question, but *know*, He will get you through it in whatever way is best for you.

I know that's a scary thought. Letting go and letting God.

The thought of joy, freedom, and potential sets the bar high for the standard of your life. Sometimes we cling to our self-destruction as an excuse to live in a way that's comfortable and easy. Admitting you could put more effort into being the best version of yourself seems like saying what's been done to you didn't matter or was okay. But whatever it is you are hanging on to doesn't identify you. Where you are in your life right now is a culmination of reactions and decisions. You don't have to take responsibility for what someone else did to hurt you, but you do have to take responsibility for the choices *you* made afterward. Letting it go doesn't mean it was okay. It means it's okay to let it go. It means releasing yourself from the control of your emotions. It means embracing your potential. It means understanding that it's not your job to make them pay, and the only person you're hurting is yourself. Most important, it means owning your decisions and taking responsibility for the quality of your life. Letting go of control requires trust. Trust requires faith. You must *know* God is good before you can lay down your life.

The problem for me was living for *His* calling and not doing what I thought was best. So for thirty years I held a tight grip on the steering wheel of my life. We all know how well that works out for us, don't we? I mean, how many of you are leading the way in your own life and feeling totally satisfied and fulfilled? I lacked discernment. Here's what's supercool, though. Every single thing we do while we wander around in the wilderness, God works out for our good. Every mistake I make molds a new message He will work through me. I took the hardest path possible to my purpose, and turns out that was exactly what was necessary for me to be the person capable of that purpose. Oddly enough. Blows my mind. The woven web of life's design is so much larger than we can see. We typically can't see past ourselves to think about what God might be working out for our future. He's the only One who knows the good that can come from the bad down the road. It's up to us to trust and follow. And you can bet the *following* part won't be easy.

You're trying to be obedient—walking through all the doors, putting yourself out there—and yet you keep on stumbling. That's usually the way it goes when you decide to have blind faith and follow whatever God puts on your heart. You're walking straight ahead, like, *I got this, I'ma get my life together, I'ma do hard things, I'ma change the world.* And the enemy's crouched down in front of you digging little holes and dropping rocks and even boulders in your path. Tripping you up, causing you to look away. And then convincing you it's your fault you're clumsy, and it had nothing to do with the landmines he put in front of your feet. Got you falling all over yourself and mad at God about it. Like, *Why didn't You warn me, Lord? I'm trying to follow You. I know You saw him setting me up, and You just let me walk right into it. Why?*

I believe it's because God can see the ripple effect of our fall. He can see that we are capable of learning and growing through it. He can see that what we take away from the stumble will be passed on to someone in desperate need of it. We are the vessels through which He works, and when God recognizes in us a heart for serving others, He will allow us to walk through the fire because He knows we will be trading in those ashes one day. He sees how we will pay it forward. Everything we do, every decision we make, every breakdown and buildup, every response we have to our circumstances, has a ripple effect bigger than us. I can hear God say, *"I love you, child, and I know what the enemy doesn't. Where I'm taking you requires you to have the character built by the fall. The enemy's plans only make you more equipped for the promised land. That's what I do, don't you see? I work for the good in all things, especially things the enemy puts in your way."*

How could you ever know just how strong you are if your strength has never been tested? How could you know that you can do hard things if everything is easy? God has a promise waiting for you, and it's bigger than you ever imagined. He needs you to be capable of receiving it. He needs you humble and willing. He needs you selfless.

CHAPTER 8

Ripple Effect

Now to him who is able to do immeasurably more than all we ask or imagine, according to his power that is at work within us, to him be glory in the church and in Christ Jesus throughout all generations, for ever and ever!
EPHESIANS 3:20-21

"I almost killed myself today."

I checked my Facebook messages and this was all I saw next to her name without having opened it yet. I hovered the mouse over the message for a few minutes before nervously clicking to open it.

"I almost killed myself today. I wanted you to know I've been struggling with so many things lately. I won't go into all of it. But I had the bottle of pills dumped into my palm, ready to swallow them all. My cell phone

notified me that you were live, and I don't know why but I felt an urge to watch. You shared your testimony and the story of your niece. I can't explain it, but as I listened I got goosebumps all over and I'm not even a religious person, but I know it was God. I've never felt anything like that before. I asked God for help so many times. But I felt like He wasn't listening. After your feed ended I put the pills back in the bottle and couldn't stop crying. For the first time, I feel like I'm not alone. My kids would have found me on the bathroom floor. So I just wanted to say thank you for listening when He tells you to speak. You might not know just how much of an impact it makes, but God saved my life through some girl I don't even know online. I'm sorry, I know that's a lot to take in from a stranger, but I wanted you to know that what you are doing matters."

There's never been a time I've spoken of my testimony in front of a live Facebook audience that I haven't felt a little nervous about the kickback I'll no doubt get. The enemy will say, *Nobody cares. Nobody wants to hear that. They only like you when you're funny. You aren't Christian enough to talk about God.* But one thing I've come to trust is that when God puts something on your heart, it's always for a reason. This Facebook follower didn't have to let me know what had happened, but God was using her to encourage me as well. We don't always know for sure if the things we're doing are making a difference. We don't always get confirmation. But I hope you will choose to believe that nothing you're prompted to do by the Lord is ever pointless.

If you knew that smiling at a stranger in the grocery store might be exactly the sign they prayed for—to know they aren't invisible—would you be more encouraged to smile? If you knew that graciously letting someone merge into your lane would prevent them from a car crash down the road, wouldn't you slow down and let them in?

Realizing the things you say and do *aren't about you* may be the key to your inspiration. How many times have you reflected back and thought about how different things could have been if it weren't for that *one* decision? Are there people out there who influenced *your* future by their own actions—who probably don't even know it? The ripple effect is less about the size of the splash and more about the waves that linger. Meaning it's not about you; it's about what you send out into the world. If you begin to have a heart for serving others, you will find yourself more capable of looking outside of your emotions. It's easier to do the right thing when we are conscious of the impact our decisions have on others.

—————

Not only so, but we also glory in our sufferings,
because we know that suffering produces perseverance;
perseverance, character; and character, hope.

ROMANS 5:3–4

Oddly enough, growing yourself means growing for others. The more we learn, the more value we have to pass on to other people. When you choose to learn from life, you accumulate more and more through your story to share with those who may currently be where you once were. And you can help them through it. There's hope in your growth. It could be joy after the loss of a loved one, a healthy life after a struggle with an eating disorder, laughter in sobriety, or peace in forgiveness. Developing a selfless attitude and thinking ahead will help you to make decisions that come full circle for your best interest as well.

It is so exciting to be who we are in Christ, because when we serve Him and follow His greatest commandment, loving God and loving others, we are able to fulfill a purpose much greater than us while serving the calling on our lives. And dang, that feels good. Living to serve others won't necessarily lead to different circumstances but will lead to an uncommon ability to maintain peace, purpose, and joy through life's ups and downs. I read an article once about a homeless man who walked miles and miles collecting change. Every day he would take what he collected and give It to a local shelter for women and children. He had nothing, but he gained so much joy in giving to others. Oh, to be that humble. I'm not that humble. This man makes me want to be a better person. We need people like him and stories like his. Bad things happen to good people, because good people show the rest of us how to handle bad things. This is a heart that God can work with. Life is a beautiful opportunity to learn, serve, grow, and sow.

Y'all know you have that one really good "bad" friend. The one you tend to get into trouble with, but they are your bestie so. . .whatever. You're trying to improve your grades, but this friend just really needs you to come out and "take a break" from your studies to day-drink strawberry daiquiris at your favorite Mexican restaurant. Five hours later you stumble into your dorm room, laughing hysterically, having forgotten all about your paper, and you sleep through the next day.

You're trying to be healthier, so this friend makes

sure to bring a batch of brownies every time she comes over and then shames you for not wanting to eat all twenty with her after ordering pizza.

You're fifteen days and six hours smoke free, but this person never fails to ask if you want to have a smoke after you finish eating the pizza and brownies, knowing that's the hardest time *not* to smoke.

I'll bet you're texting your friend right now like, "Hey, just realized you're my best bad friend. LOL."

Well, guess what—this person's gotta go.

Just kiiidding. But seriously, you can see not only how you are influenced by others, but how you just might be influencing them too.

Are you the best bad friend? If so, then why? Why don't you want to see people you care about becoming better versions of themselves? More than likely it's because you aren't ready to break your own bad habits, and they are your favorite person to self-destruct with. Getting your life together always requires sacrificing things that feel good to the flesh. Things that feel good right now often do deep damage later. For the moment it might be fun, but there's only ever regret after the party. If you don't expect much of yourself or don't feel you are worthy of a higher quality of life, you'll never level up. You will accept mediocrity and drag as many people down with you as you can. If you have a "bad" friend like this, be honest with her and encourage her. If she wants to stay the same, don't let it keep you from making a change. Let the knowledge that "this life isn't about you but what you leave behind" mean more to you than continuing a life less than you are created for.

And parents, guess what, your kids are watching you. You already know that, but just in case you think it's totally harmless to have them lie to their teacher about how their little sister ripped up their reading log when you actually just threw it away with the week's worth of school papers you never read, you are wrong. Dangit. Cough, cough. I may or may not have drawn that example from my own life. But don't even act like y'all don't know how quickly those papers pile up!

All jokes aside, it's the little things—the sneaky little things that seem harmless—that snowball years later into character flaws we find really hard to break. Honesty, for example, doesn't only apply to the *big* lies. I'll give you some little examples of how God worked in me on the small stuff. . . .

Have you ever taken three children to the grocery store? My girls are nine, seven, and four years old. Now, I just so happen to be blessed with pretty well-behaved children (for the most part). *However,* there is something about the Targets that transforms them into whining, fussing, touching-everything-we-walk-past, selective-hearing little psychos. I sat in the car just praying and pumping myself up. Pre-warning them of the consequences they would pay if I ended up having to have a come-apart in front of all the classy, Lululemon-wearing, put-together moms. Things started off fairly smooth. My youngest didn't fight me on sitting in the buggy (that's "shopping cart" for you northerners). We passed right by the one-dollar trinkets without any touching. They didn't whine when I detoured at the "way too young for me, but I'm in denial" crop tops and cutoffs section to browse for way too long before giving up on my teenage daydream. But then we hit the ten-minute mark, and the consequences I had listed out earlier began to seem totally worth a mommy mental breakdown. I think some days it's just pure entertainment for the kids. I mean, I know I take great joy in rehashing all the times my mom went bat-crap crazy on us. My siblings and I laugh until we cry and can't breathe talking about it. Well, y'all, we all pay for our raisin' at some point, and my mama just chuckles when I tell her my Targets toddler tantrum stories.

By the time I get to the exit doors, I have boss baby thrown over my shoulder so she doesn't get hit by a car and die, which has destroyed her good time. My middle child is guilt-tripping me because I told her exactly twelve days ago I might get her something from the store, and today was apparently supposed to be that day. And my oldest is pouting because her legs are tired, but she takes up too much space in the buggy to sit in there with the groceries. Plus she makes it too heavy to steer with my one available hand as the other is keeping a flailing, grunting, tiny human from racing across the parking lot into the tire of an old lady backing up without looking. I'm done. I've lost control of my attitude, and I'm sweaty. Partly as a response to judgy stares from parents who have it all figured out (or childless teenagers who think they have it all figured out because they read a lot of Facebook parenting articles). Partly because I need to work out more. Also a little because it's all my fault for not going to the store earlier when they were at school. *Doh.*

I told you all of that to get to this. I get all of them in the car and begin to put the groceries in the back. Squeezed into the tiny space between the front child seat and the larger part of the buggy is a bottle of mouthwash that didn't get scanned. *Nooooooo. Please, no. Okay, no, I didn't see it. Nope, I don't even know it's there. It's not like it's expensive. I was not trying to steal it. If I was, I wouldn't have just purchased a hundred dollars' worth of other stuff. It was an innocent mistake. They should have noticed. It's not my fault. I can't be expected to drag all three of my kids back in there just to pay for this one little item.* Y'all, this inner monologue went on in my driver's seat for about five minutes, which might as well have been twenty to three ticked-off kids post-grocery shopping with Mom.

There was a time I would have left that parking lot and never thought about it again. But on this day, despite all the reasons it wasn't a big deal, it felt like a big deal. I told the girls we accidentally took something without paying, unbuckled my toddler, walked back into the store, got in the back of the line, and waited patiently. Blew the cashier's mind. When we got back into the car, my oldest said, "You did the right thing, Mom." An example was set that day by a convicted mommy who operates outside of her emotions. God gave me that gift. It may feel like a chain, but it's actually freedom. A freedom from making wrong choices influenced by feelings. Sometimes it's a gift that inconveniences me and drives me nuts. I argue with it and rebuke it as if it's actually the devil. But these are the little things. The teeny tiny decisions that shape not only who we are, but also the little ones who watch us.

My girls saw honesty in me that day. They learned that honesty matters, even when the world tells them it's no big deal. They saw me do something a lot of people wouldn't have done. I hope that is what they carry with them as they grow. Not the death-stare in the store, but doing what was right even though it was annoying. The ripple effect will carry through their memory of a moment Mama did what was right when she didn't want to. Truly, that's something I constantly want to work on—operating outside of emotions. If you can learn not to base your decisions on your emotions, you'll be capable of making the right choices despite how you feel. For example, taking care of yourself when you reallllly don't want to. Taking care of yourself will impact those around you in ways you may not realize. I mean, how many times have you felt inspired to be healthier just from a simple story shared online of a mom of six battling depression and winning because she decided there was nothing selfish about making her mental, emotional, and physical health a priority. When she needs time, she takes it. She doesn't even give her husband an option. She says, "Take them. I'm driving around alone for ten minutes." She knows what she needs to be a better mom, and therefore, her health *is* their health. Before you know it, you've logged off, tossed the toddler onto Dad's napping face, hit the road with windows down and zero guilt, and returned a brand-new woman ready to serve dinner, play a game, tackle bathtime splash madness, and *maybe* Netflix and "not chill"? Who knows, the possibilities are endless. The ripple effect, y'all. She'll never know her story may have just given you exactly what you need to make a change. That's how it works.

Let's take a detour here, because it's so important that we get this. A massive contributor to unhappiness is a lack of self-worth. We can easily cover it up with excuses, but deep down our misery is built on the lie that we don't deserve to be happy. Bouncing off chapter 1 where we talked about the lies the enemy tells us and the way he uses the world to do it. . .he knows what happens when a person sees value in their life. And you know what happens when you live outside of your emotions? You do what needs to be done whether you want to or not. Your feelings are heavily influenced by uncontrollable outside circumstances. Each day you have no idea what might happen that you didn't anticipate. Someone may say something hurtful to you. It might be snowing when it was *supposed* to be spring. (*Uggghhh.* LOL). A coworker could call in sick leaving you to work a double shift. Your car could decide it doesn't want to go anywhere. The *huge* insurance bill might show up in the mail. Your credit card number might be stolen (by what I can only imagine is a twenty-two-year-old girl capable of blowing seven hundred dollars at Ulta). Your kid may decide to inform you—on the way to school—that you were supposed to help them build a robot for a huge percentage of their grade, and it's due *today!* The bank may think your late-night shopping on QVC was fraud and cut off your credit card without telling you. . .and you don't discover it until Saturday—in line at the grocery store—when the bank is *closed.* Meaning you have to relive your embarrassing childhood poverty and walk away from all your groceries as you loudly announce it's the bank's fault and you *do* have money. Lots of money, in fact. Enough to buy all *their* groceries too.

Y'all see what I'm saying, right? *Anything* can happen, good or bad. So do you want your peace and joy wrapped up in your emotions? Do you want to base your decisions on whether your day goes exactly as planned? And mamas, don't get mad at me, but you gotta stop it with the need to feel motivated or inspired in order to take care of yourself. That just ain't always gonna be the case. If you truly want to be the best version of yourself, it's gonna have to happen amid plenty of no-good, crappy days. Life will *never* get out of your way and make things easier. But when you understand who you truly are in Christ and how much He loves you—when you understand just how valuable you really are to Him—you'll begin to *embrace* a lifestyle that requires effort. Believe me, it takes effort to be mentally, spiritually, and physically healthy. (Your reading this book right now is already an effort, and I'm so proud of you for it!)

Sisters in Christ, do not use putting God first as a reason you can't take care of yourself. You weren't meant to live in misery. Exhausted, stressed, overwhelmed, and joyless is *not* what Christ died to give you. He left His Spirit so you could feel peace and joy in a fallen world. But you gotta care about yourself enough to pour into yourself each day. That means strengthening your relationship with Him each day, first and foremost. Just hang out with Him. Study the Word. Pray—it's simply a conversation with God. Prayer won't always lead to an immediate and obvious answer, but it helps you discern the right choices for the path He wants you on. The closer you get to Him, the more you'll find that making yourself a priority is not selfish; it's *necessary*. How are you gonna be a vessel through which He sends out a ripple of light and love if you're moody all the dang time, never feeling good, always tired, anxious, depressed, and unhappy?

There's a difference between obsessing over yourself, being vain, being selfish, and simply taking care of yourself. How would you feel if your children walked around unable to see just how amazing they really are? And where do you think they would learn that? The ripple effect, girl.

I don't want my daughters to grow up thinking it's a bad thing to care about your health. I don't want them thinking it's normal and acceptable to criticize themselves and expect little of their lives because that's the example I set. And God doesn't want that for you either. He has compassion and love for you. He wants you to thrive. He wants you to succeed. He wants you to love the vessel in which He placed your soul. Most importantly, He wants you living out your life's purpose.

Your life's purpose will always be selflessness, and taking care of yourself is paradoxically crucial to becoming selfless. In the wisdom-laced words of Elle from the movie *Legally Blonde*, "Working out releases endorphins. Endorphins make you happy. Happy people just don't shoot their husbands. They just don't." Just like happy women don't tear each other down, happy moms don't snap at their children so quickly, and happy wives might not throw all their husband's clothes in the hallway when he leaves the toilet seat up. What's good for you is good for those around you. You can't pour joy from a stressed-out cup. So I don't wanna hear it with the "Well, I'm just keeping my priorities in order." Nowhere does scripture say that putting yourself dead last is how you best serve the Lord. Are you honestly the best mom you can be when you are tired and moody? I mean, even the healthiest of us lose our minds at the 275th "Mom Mom Mom" by 8:00 a.m. So when you're overloaded and unhappy, it only takes repeating "Get your shoes on" twice to put you in the midst of a psychopathic mental breakdown. Y'all know I ain't lying.

Here's some of the best advice I could give anyone who's ready to be healthy and happy. Look at your body as if it is one of your children. Be kind to it. Don't hate it. That's not fair. Your thoughts about your body are a reflection of the way you treat it, so *stop* saying negative things about it. Stop calling yourself disgusting and ugly. See your body for what it is—an incredible, capable, powerful vessel that has put up with years and years of neglect and abuse from you. Love on it. Nurture it. Give it time to react. If you begin taking care of yourself for the right reasons, you'll be less likely to give up and get down on yourself when you become impatient. Take care of yourself for one reason and one reason only— *because it's good.* It's good for your life. It's good for your spirit. It's good for your family. It's essential to your marriage.

Wanna be the very best wife you can be? Patient,

understanding, capable of fun, interested in intimacy? Let me ask: how's that going when you're overloaded, exhausted, sluggish, insecure, and stressed out? I tell y'all, my husband can't even ask me a super-simple question without me losing my temper when I'm not in a good place....

Husband: "How was your day?"

Me: "What's *that* supposed to mean? *How was my day.* Are you serious? How do you think it was? How would you feel if you had over a million things to do and your spouse had the nerve to ask you what you did all day? How was *your* day not having to think about anyone or anything other than yourself?"

Husband: "That's not what I said. Just wanted to know how your day was."

Me: "Oh, I *know* what you meant by it."

Sound familiar?

Y'all, I swear I had an all-out come-apart on this man one time when he clipped his nails in my bed. I'm gonna save the whole story for my next book, but let's just say *everything* he owned wound up in the closet, and I cried and laughed and went to sleep. Sorrrrry, I know that's torture, but guess you'll have to get book number two. Mwahahahaha.

When I make the choice not to take time for myself to pray, read, journal, exercise, meditate, and sit in the quiet to enjoy some alone time, everyone around me suffers the ripple effect from it.

When I was young, I was a tomboy. I hated Barbies and dresses, loved dirt, loved all things sports, and spent my whole day shooting the basketball, tossing a ball up in the air, racing my bike, or just running. I was extremely competitive, which resulted in many, *many* fights between my little brother and me. It never even crossed my mind that I could be on an actual sports team, because my siblings and I just didn't get to do things like that. I knew we didn't have any money. I had been told *no* enough to figure out there was no point in even asking. But one day my mom and I were in the car when she said, "Carolanne, would you like to play softball this summer?"

My heart leaped out of my chest, and I screamed, *"Yes yes yes yes yes!"* I was straight-up giddy, y'all. For the first time in my life, I felt excited because I was about to have something of my own. I don't know how my mom came up with the money to pay for registration, but I also needed cleats and a glove. This must have been so stressful for my mama. Something as simple as signing up your kid for a sports team was a serious financial stressor for us. A friend of my mom's from church, Ramona Daniels, was kind enough to give Mom her glove to give to me. (Gah,

I'm gonna try not to cry, but I guess it doesn't matter since y'all can't see me.) This glove meant the world to me. It wasn't *just* a glove. It was *mine*. Probably the only material thing I owned that I actually cared enough about to really take care of. I slathered it in Vaseline, put a ball in it, and tied it up. Slept with it every night. This was my leather ticket to an hour of freedom in the dirt. An hour to do all the things I loved without worry of what might be happening outside of that ballpark. It was my safe space. I couldn't get enough. Funny thing is, as good as I thought I was in my granny's front yard all alone throwing tennis balls at the fence, when it came to real softball, I started off pretty terrible. I had no idea how to throw, catch, or hit. I also had this weird tendency to get hit in the head with the ball. (Maybe that's why I'm so goofy.) At my very first practice, a little girl standing next to me threw the ball right at my head instead of to her partner. But I didn't care.

I was so eager to learn the game. I wasn't the best player out on the field, but I had to be dragged off that field when practice was over. I listened, and I applied. I wanted to be the best. Truthfully, I wanted to be needed. So I put that glove to good use. And that glove grew up with me. It missed a lot of balls until it *never* missed a ball. It fell apart on me more than once. But I always managed to tie it back together and focus on the next play.

Many times this glove kept me from ruining my life. There were several summers in high school when I tried hard to self-destruct. Smoking and drinking. It was always the glove and the thought that I could lose the opportunity to play softball that straightened me up. As a matter of fact, the only reason I graduated high school was so I wouldn't miss the state tournament. For real. I sat in my creative writing class half an hour before the bus left for state, finishing a paper that I had to pass in order to play in the game. I wrote the whole paper in twenty minutes, under the glare of an annoyed teacher. . .and I danced right out the door when she sighed the words, "You passed." I was always pushing boundaries. *Always.*

At the state tournament, a lot of college scouts were watching us play. I had given up hope that I'd get a scholarship. I thought I was good enough, but my high school coach didn't. I was one of the best outfielders of any school there. The best glove. But my batting average was horrible. My coach wouldn't let me bat left handed (slap). I believed I'd do so great from that side too. I saw the ball better, and I was *fast.* A result of all those years running around the track by my granny's house.

Little did I know, God had plans for me and that

glove passed down by Mrs. Ramona. One play. It all came down to one play. I caught a ball deep in center field. The runner on third decided to try to run home after I caught it. (This was my favorite thing in the whole world. I loved being challenged like that.) I reared back and threw a line shot from deep center field right to the chest of my catcher who tagged the runner as she slid into home. *Out!*

And guess what? A coach named Ricky Howell just so happened to turn and see the ball zip from the outfield to home. He wanted to know who did that. Turns out he was the new head coach at a small junior college, Bevill State (BSCC). They had never won a single softball game, and he was looking to build a new team. Specifically, a scrappy team. Kids he could work with to grow, push, and challenge. He saw that in me. So I received a full paid scholarship to BSCC, as well as the gift of confidence that my life had possibility.

On the very first day of college ball practice, my old glove crumbled to pieces. It had given me all it had, and I was devastated. It was like a piece of me passed away. My coach was kind enough to give me his glove "until I could get a new one." It was a nice, fancy glove. Truthfully, I'm sure he knew I'd never get another one. Coach Howell was like a father to me. He saw something in me. He challenged me, set expectations for me, and trusted me as a leader. I became the absolute best athlete I could possibly be because of him. But I also felt encouraged that my life had possibility. Coach never took it easy on us, but he always acted in love. And the team respected him. I watched every player on my team race to their full potential. But none of us was able to reach it without being completely broken first. We would stay out on that field until the sun went down, and then we would pull up cars and turn on the headlights until every single one of us cleanly caught and threw one hundred balls each. Until every one of us was a sweaty, filthy, bloody mess. Picture us out there. On the verge of giving up after missing the ninety-ninth ball and having to start back at one. But out of nowhere, the team would catch a second wind and rally behind their mate. We may have been a mess, but we were cheering, laughing, and in it *together*.

Coach Howell changed *who* we were. He made us better human beings, and I will always be grateful to have been led to this time of my life. Ramona had no idea that the gift of that glove would change my life. I went on to earn a four-year scholarship to Faulkner University (my batting average went way up when I became a lefty slapper) and became the first person in my family to graduate college with a bachelor's degree in English. (Never thought I'd use it, but here I am a decade later writing a book.)

Coach Howell will never know the place he has in my heart. The character he instilled in me remains even today. Our scrappy little team of nine, yes, nine, went on to become second in state that year, which was a huge leap from zero wins years before. We were the underdog nobody saw coming. *And* we were the Bears! (Ya know, like the movie *Bad News Bears*. If you haven't seen it, we can't be friends.)

Because of my poverty, I needed a glove. And it was the kindness behind Ramona giving me hers that gave me a whole new life and motivation to work hard. It was the absence of a dad that gave me a deep appreciation for what Coach Howell was pouring into me. *The ripple effect.* Good can come from bad, and none of us knows just how much we mean in the lives of others. *Everything* you do matters. And oddly enough. . .it's the things that make life harder that often develop the greatest character.

CHAPTER 9

MISTAKES AND GRACE

"My grace is sufficient for you, for my power is made perfect in weakness." Therefore I will boast all the more gladly about my weaknesses, so that Christ's power may rest on me.
2 CORINTHIANS 12:9

I mentioned earlier that there wasn't a single time I gave my body to my boyfriend without feeling bad about it. . .like it was just wrong. That includes sleeping with my now-husband before we were married. We hadn't even discussed important things—like marriage, kids, what we wanted out of life, or the qualities we saw our spouse having. We liked each other. . .*a lot*. But we were so young. We started dating when I was twenty, and I went to college a few months after that. So for four years we maintained a long-distance relationship, and we liked it. When we saw each other, we were ecstatic to be in each other's presence. (A little too ecstatic.) He had my heart, but if I'm being honest with myself—and with you—no matter how right it *felt*, we weren't ready to act like we were married. Everything was fun, careless, and irresponsible. I now know just how childish you can be, even in your twenties, when you feel like you are adulting so hard.

Two months after I graduated from college and returned home, I became pregnant with our first daughter. Was that ideal? No. He was in a band, we lived in a band house, I was a waitress, and we flat-out weren't ready. But when that tenth pregnancy test said, *Yes, you are pregnant. You can stop taking tests now. You're going to get dehydrated,* my whole life changed. I grew in a way I needed to and honestly don't think I would have without my baby. She woke us up. She wasn't a mistake; she was an awakening. She was everything we needed. We needed to care about something more than ourselves. We needed a reality check. With her little eyes watching, I wanted to set a better example. So, just like that, she made me a better person.

I know we all have something we'd like to go back in time and do differently. There are some experiences I'd be tempted to take back, for sure. But I don't want to think about the things I'd have to live without today, had everything gone right for me in the past. I've read somewhere that if nothing changes, nothing changes. That baby changed us. We have been so blessed with each of our daughters. Not one of them was planned, but we can't imagine our lives without them. I don't wanna know what that would even look like. Have you ever seen the movie *The Family Man*? Nicholas Cage gets a glimpse of what life would look like had he made a different choice. He gets to know a family and a life that "could have been." And just when he falls in love with his kids, the glimpse is over and he goes back to the life many people dream of: all the money in the world, and no one to share it with. But knowing what he could have had makes the fancy clothes, limo, one-night stands, and hot-shot job a lot less appealing.

———

There isn't a choice I've made that can't be used to demonstrate God's grace. That's the beauty in our mistakes. And I have learned to embrace my mistakes, because they always teach me valuable lessons moving forward to whatever lies ahead. I now know I *cannot* write at home. Even when my husband is in the house, the only words in my children's vocabulary are "Mom," "Mama," "Ma," "Hey, Mom," "Maaaaama," "Mommy," and "I'm hungry." I learned that I need headphones, uplifting music, and to be completely alone. Trying to focus in the midst of chaos taught me that…I can't.

Of course, there have been plenty of days of doubt and feeling like I'm doing things all wrong. But this is what I fall back on: there *will* come a day when everything I've learned from my failures will be used for a massive success. I got yelled at—spit-spraying-my-nose yelled at—more than a few times doing door-to-door sales before I learned how to approach people. But before long, I was a top sales rep in the company. The meanest people taught me the most. I trust in God's plan for me. And I trust Romans 8:28 when it says that God works for the good in *all* things for those called according to *His* purpose. So long as my heart desires to serve Him, I know He'll take anything I do wrong and make it right for the calling He has placed on my life. It doesn't always make sense, and I don't always feel like I'm winning, but there's so much to be learned from losing.

This is what makes life interesting. This is what makes life beautiful. This is what's so exciting about potential. When you embrace mistakes, they become building blocks in the creation of your better character. You will find yourself able to pursue life with more courage than fear. Girls, this is what it's all about. Being able to welcome *every* aspect of life.

Being open to never-ending possibilities. Tapping into the fruit of the Holy Spirit so that your wilderness *is* your promised land. Here's the thing: when you feel like you just don't know what God's doing in your life and nothing makes sense, look around and ask questions. *Who is around me? What can be learned from this? Is there a way for me to bless someone right now? What do I have to be grateful for?* You must be humble and have a willingness to be taught in the midst of a situation in which you aren't very happy. You won't always know what's going on and why. I really had to give up needing to know *why* all the time. Wanting to know why steals too much peace from your spirit as you seek answers you may never get. For me, "God is good," and that's all I need to know. My love for Him isn't conditional. I know only what I need to know, and I've accepted that.

Right at this moment, maybe you wish you could change something about your life. But I want you to remember that even what you see as your mistakes are part of a plan that is better for you than anything you could put together yourself. It's a choice you make to live and learn. You can't trade ashes for beauty if you've never been burned. So embrace the flames. They are necessary to your character and your calling. I know that who I am has been shaped by everything I've been through. Your wilderness is where the lessons are learned, so when you feel lost in wrong choices, tune out the world's voices and take a look around. There's always a reason for where you are. When you stray from the path God has you on, He'll just give you something new and useful to bring with you when you come back. Sometimes I find myself struggling and I don't even know why. I will just feel nervous, anxious, down, and depressed. I've learned that it's in these seasons that I'm receiving some valuable lessons to pay forward. I've learned not to let my emotions trick me into believing God is finished with me. Don't ever let guilt, regret, or losing your way keep you parked in your pain. It might take a day, it might take a week, but the pain will pass. Looking back, you'll be able to see what work was being done in you.

Truthfully, a life without mistakes is a life without growth. So no more trying to be perfect. Step away from the better wife/mother/woman blogs for a moment and remember that none of us are perfect. Sometimes you just need to vent. Sometimes your kids drive you nuts. Sometimes your house is wrecked and you just don't care. Trying to achieve an unrealistic standard will only stress you out, because it's just not possible.

You learn so much about yourself from your

choices, and knowing who you are is essential to becoming the best version of yourself. For example, I know that if I don't set boundaries, I will become overwhelmed and stressed. I don't do well with too many plates to balance. Just like that story about when I waited tables that I told y'all. My clumsy self will 100 percent slip on butter and wind up facedown in a pile of broken glass. I've had to learn the hard way that the more things I say yes to, the more anxious I feel. Then I start to become easily agitated, impatient, exhausted, joyless, and sad.

I also know I'm a stress eater. I have a tendency to try to binge-eat my depression away. The eating is a distraction. As long as I'm "busy" eating, I can avoid dealing with the overwhelming responsibilities I don't feel capable of taking care of. But then the food runs out, I feel sick to my stomach and ashamed of myself, and the to-do list still stands. Knowing this helps me remember to say no when I need to.

I know what it feels like when I give too much of myself, and it leaves me no good to anybody. I've learned to focus on the calling God has given me and trust my gut when something sounds great but will distract me from what *He* wants me doing. How did I learn this, you ask? *By doing all of it all wrong.* When I'm walking in a circle, with more responsibilities than I can handle and unsure where to even begin, I know I've said yes to too many things. Doing it all wrong gives me wisdom, moving forward, to do it right.

By the way, whatever it is you've been called to do is where you should place your focus. And when you aren't focused on trying to avoid mistakes, you'll be free to enjoy the journey God has for you. One thing that often happens as you strengthen your gifts in pursuit of your calling is that people swoop in to try to take bits of those gifts for their own benefit. If you say yes to too many people, you'll be left too drained to tackle your top priorities. That's a mistake I've definitely made and learned from. For example, I know God wants me writing and speaking. Those are two things I know without a shadow of a doubt I'm supposed to do. But bouncing off the sidelines of writing and speaking come requests for videos, shout-outs, collaborations, one-on-one conversations, product reviews, new videos, "make me laugh," "return my message," "reply to my comment," etc., and before I know it I'm so busy doing all these other things to please people, I've made no time for the *two* things I've been called for.

Don't let distractions disguised as opportunities, or a desire to please people, keep you from staying on the path God has set before you. Pray for discernment. *Sometimes* discernment comes out of mistakes. You've heard it before, but fail forward. When I fell on my face that day waiting tables, I felt like such a loser. But I needed to. Without the blood-warming, heart-racing, embarrassed feeling of that day, I wouldn't have made a change.

———

When I was in high school, everyone told me I should run track. I was really fast in softball and basketball, so I figured I'd crush it. As the *Saturday Night Live* church lady sarcastically says, "Isn't *that* special?"

I had no idea what I was getting myself into. During the very first practice, we had a relay race. Well, *they* had a relay race, but *I* had a rude awakening. They made me anchor, y'all. Like whyyyyy? I'm standing next to the other anchor looking like a hobbit. He was about two feet taller than me, long and lanky like a graceful gazelle. His legs were nothing but bone and muscle. He looked like an adult Olympic runner. I thought, *Well, I'm scrappy and fast, so I got this.*

Our team was an entire lap ahead by the time I got the baton. I was halfway around the track and thought, *Why is this track so much bigger than it looks?* Then, out of my peripheral, I saw Gary Gazelle galloping gracefully toward me. Every leap he effortlessly took equaled six of my stupid little steps. He was white lightnin' without even tryin'. I was giving it all I had and about tapped out. The closer he got to me, the more I panicked. Anyone who knows me knows I *hate* losing. Especially at something I know I'm good at. So when he sailed right past me without even breathing heavy, I turned it on. Full speed. Everything I had. I was pushing as hard as I possibly could just to barely stay on his heels, and we still had half a track to go, if y'all can imagine this. Him gliding smoothly ahead with me left behind, puttering out and unable to breathe. By the time I crawled across the finish line, he had already gotten a drink, rested, and stretched for his next race. When I finally made it, everyone clapped and cheered and giggled hysterically. They knew he was going to smoke me all along. The coach put me as anchor on purpose to teach me a hard lesson.

Many times in my life, I've had to make a fool of myself before understanding that I don't always know what I'm doing. Over and over I've had to sprint ahead before it was time, putter out, and almost die in order to realize that God's timing will take me there so much faster. His steps look slow, but they are strong, steady, and graceful. My steps are too much, too fast, too soon. I always have to give in to Him before I can win. He *is* your second wind.

Naturally, the next thing the coaches had me try was cross country. Seeing as I'm a sprinter, I went into it feeling like *nur*. But I wanted to at least try. Once again, deep down I thought maybe I'd come out the gate, blow everyone away, and win. Ahhh, isn't that precious? I told y'all I'm stubborn.

The first meet I ran started off okay. I didn't go too fast too soon. I knew it was a long run. But I really hated having to allow people to pass me while keeping my own pace. Oooooh, can we apply *that* to life right quick. I'ma say that again: *one of the hardest things in the race of life is keeping God's pace while others pass you by.* Can I get an amen? You gotta trust He knows better. What He's doing through someone else is for them. His plan for you will happen in His timing. It's a test I've failed many times over.

About halfway through this long-distance meet, I really started to hurt. I started feeling like I truly couldn't take another step. My stomach was cramping, my lungs were done, and I had zero energy left. As I was bent over about to give up, I felt an arm loop into mine and pull me forward. My sister's friend ran up from behind me and just took me with her. As done as my body was, my spirit was lifted by the kindness she showed me. If she was going to slow herself down to keep me from quitting, I was gonna muster up the gas to keep going. I fed off her energy for about half a mile, and then out of nowhere all the inspiration and motivation my teammate gave me kicked in and I took off up the final hill. When I got to the top, I could see the finish line. I was filled with excitement, and I went into a dead sprint all the way down and across the finish line.

There's something so powerful about an encouraged spirit. It will carry your tired, hurting, doubtful flesh uphill and across the finish line. That's what life is like when you have a relationship with Jesus. There are plenty of times you'll feel like quitting. Your body will be in pain, and your brain will tell you it can't go on. But as you're bent over feeling broken, the Holy Spirit will come out of nowhere and lock arms with you. He will drag you forward until you catch your second wind. He will fill you with a peace, hope, and joy you didn't think was possible. He carried me through my saddest days after we lost Ansley. He gave me strength to continue telling her story. And He will renew *your* spirit and fill *your* heart with belief. Belief that you can do all things through Christ who is your strength when your flesh is weak. Trust me, it will kick in at just the right time. Keep your eyes on the finish line.

———————

But he said to me, "My grace is sufficient for you,
for my power is made perfect in weakness."
Therefore I will boast all the more gladly about my
weaknesses, so that Christ's power may rest on me.
That is why, for Christ's sake, I delight in weaknesses,

in insults, in hardships, in persecutions, in difficulties.
For when I am weak, then I am strong.
2 CORINTHIANS 12:9-10

Dang. I'm gonna be honest. I've known of that scripture for a while. But reading it right now really hits home. If we are never weak, we will never get a taste of His strength. We have to learn that He is enough for us. We usually discover that in our wilderness. When we are lost, wandering, huffing, puffing, and thinking of quitting. I don't know about you, but I will boast *gladly* about my weaknesses. I will look forward to the many lessons awaiting me. I will not play it safe. I'm willing to make mistakes. Because I know that I know that I know *that I know*, Christ's power will rest on me. Will lock arms with me, drag me along, and lift me up. For *His* sake, I'll *delight* in insults. Oh boy. Scripture is preaching here. I will *delight* in insults. I will not argue with Facebook trolls. I will not tell them what I think of them. I will not let them steal my joy. I will *delight* in my haters because they poke at the weakness in my flesh and give Christ a chance to show Himself in me. Ohhhhh, that is good. Come on now. I will *delight* in hardships. *Delight* means a strong feeling of pleasure, happiness, or satisfaction. I will be satisfied when times get tough. Why? Because I have the joy of the

Lord! He fills up my spirit when my flesh is tapped out. For when I am put in situations that make me weak, *He* will make me strong, y'all. You'd better believe it!

So let the Lord rain on your parade when your pride needs to be washed away. Let Him shower you with grace. He is sufficient. He is enough. You don't need to feel ashamed. You don't need to earn His love. You don't need to work off any wrongs you've done. You can't run from imperfection, but you can learn from frustration. From regret comes restoration. Take it from me. Speedy Gonzales humiliated by Twinkle Toes. The spots where I fall are where I learn the most.

———

Do you know how a muscle grows? You challenge it with weight that's just a little bit heavier than what it's currently capable of bearing. As you push through, it leaves tiny tears. When the workout is over, it's what you *feed* your body that either fills in those tears, leading to growth and change, or does nothing for you. The tears heal back to the same size they were before. So what you fuel your body with afterward is either fruitful or wasteful.

When you feel you're being stretched and tested beyond your strength, you have a choice to make.

Are you gonna feed your flesh or your spirit? You can respond with self-destruction, learning zero lessons and wasting your mistakes. Or you can strap on your armor and fill up on the Word. You can feed your spirit with praise and prayer. You can allow God to fill in those tears, to strengthen your character and make you better.

We've talked about knowing who you are and writing it down. Now's the time to *speak* it! Now's the time to *claim* it. This is how you fight. *Pray* and *praise* are action verbs. So when the enemy is telling you to give up on your health, go show him what's up by crushing your workout. When he says you can't run that mile, put on your sneakers. When he says you can't write that book, put your pen to paper.

Do You Want to Change or Stay the Same?

I know you have something you'd like to change. An area you'd like to improve in your life. So tell me. . .what are you doing about it? Because "Listen, Linda" (remember that kid?), you cannot do the things you've always done and make any progress. You've seen those before-and-after pictures of people who started taking care of themselves, and over time they became the "girl on the right."

If you took a picture of yourself right now, what would you see staring back at you? What are you harboring? What would come through in that photo? Now, imagine what your *after* would look like. Would you look happily at peace, healthy, and renewed? What do you think happens in the time between the *before* and *after*? It's a process to get there, but the girl on the right doesn't make the same decisions as the girl on the left. She doesn't respond to life the same way. She doesn't make choices based on emotions. When life gets tough, she digs in her heels and learns from the hardships. She doesn't expect everything to go right. And she embraces the fight. She knows transformation hurts. But love is pain—loving life, loving yourself, loving the struggles, and loving the hustle are all a part of what makes your transformation beautiful. The girl on the right has learned. She has exchanged her burns for beauty. She makes mistakes, but she moves forward with grace.

Sister, you can get there. See it, speak it, believe it. He has plans to prosper you! You can't even imagine how God can use all the baggage you're dragging behind you. If the girl from *before* let herself stay stuck in PARK every time things went wrong, what does the girl from the *after* photo do? She listens, she learns, and she knows that when she prays, she is heard. She carries no chains. She knows her mistakes are always followed by His grace.

CHAPTER 10

TURNING CHAINS INTO REINS

His divine power has given us everything we need for a godly life through our knowledge of him who called us by his own glory and goodness. Through these he has given us his very great and precious promises, so that through them you may participate in the divine nature, having escaped the corruption in the world caused by evil desires.

2 PETER 1:3–4

You made it to chapter 10 with me! You're my favorite. I've been asked over and over again what my book is about. At times it has been tough to answer that question. It's about pretty much *all the things*, right? Ha! But mostly, I want you to be encouraged to know that it is *all the things* that have made you feel unworthy, less than, different, ashamed, insecure, and insignificant that actually make you exactly who you need to be as an individual in order to fulfill your purpose. I've been poor, molested, bullied, and overwhelmed by loss just like you. If you've ever felt like an outsider, so have I. If you've felt unaccepted or unwelcomed, so have I. If you've felt you weren't talented enough, pretty enough, smart enough, or rich enough to be worth loving, I understand. I get it.

I always thought the things that were happening to me were happening because I wasn't deserving of a normal life. Particularly me. Like I somehow slipped through the cracks. I didn't realize I was worthy of a calling *because* of the things that were happening to me. I didn't know Jesus then. I didn't understand that what He did was all for me—and you. Particularly me. Particularly you.

Take it personally. Jesus was an outcast. He was a weirdo. He hung out with the most sinful people and demonstrated *through them* the level of change His love could bring. He loved the unlovable. He carried that cross, took on that burden, and suffered that pain because living in this fallen world would cause all of us great suffering. So He took it on in the flesh so that our spirits could be set free from it one day. He suffered the consequences of every bad decision each of us would ever make. And He left us the gift of His Spirit to give us peace, joy, and an ability to navigate through our own hardships back to the promises of God. To give us an understanding that only *His*

Spirit could have because of what He did for us on that cross.

Every wrong choice I made caused God that much more rejoicing when He caught up to me. When I realized the truth—that little ol' countrified, molested, poor, broken me was important enough to have been sought after every second of my life—I wept. I sobbed. I fell to my knees in amazement that it's *true*. He loves me. I matter. I'm not lost. See ya later, chains of shame.

———

Sister, we all come from different places and backgrounds, and we all handle ourselves differently. But something is heavy on my heart. We say we pray for those who feel the most hopeless to be found. But are you rejoicing in the salvation of those you consider beneath you (addicts, thieves, etc.), or are you irritated, maybe even jealous, that God loves them too? That He seeks them as much as He seeks you? Do you realize that maybe the wicked aren't those so obviously rebelling against good, but those who stand on their pedestal judging from above showing *zero* love? Ouch. That hurts me too, because when someone hurts us, it's so hard to love them. But when someone has been the lowest of the low, it's that much more thrilling to see God change them.

I want to ask you a hard question: Have you ever

been condescending and criticizing from the comfort of your church circles? I'm not getting down on church or conservative Christians. I love you. I grew up with you. There's nothing I love more than the celebration and energy of praise streaming from the sanctuary of a Southern Baptist church. I'm just saying, as a *whole*, we need to watch the tone behind our words. The truth is, our sole purpose as Christians is to bring people to Christ, not chase them away with their tail tucked between their legs feeling ashamed of themselves.

I think families like mine can make the well-to-do crowd a little nervous. People who wear their mess on their sleeve, instead of tucking it away and pretending, can make others feel uncomfortable. We are reminders that God's love isn't dependent upon good works, good looks, a good act, or an ability to recite the Bible front to back. You can't put on a show for the Lord. He sees you. He sees you behind closed doors. He knows your heart, and He *loves* you *as you are*. Just like He loves sociable Sandra from the wrong side of town who sleeps around. Just like He loves buzzed Billy at the bar hiding from his demons in a pint of whiskey. Just like He loved my mama. A struggling, divorced single mother with three kids who wandered into the church from the trailer park against all the looks and judgment she would face. My mama said these exact words:

"Twenty-eight years ago, my life was a mess. Newly divorced with three little kids depending on me for everything. I didn't know what I was going to do. But I knew that my kids deserved better than what I was giving them. I began to feel a pull. Stronger than anything I had ever felt before. A longing for God. We would drive down highway 78, and I felt a pull to that big church on the hill. I didn't want to be that poor pitiful lady dragging in the three pitiful little kids. I knew people who went there, but even worse was that some of them knew me. But I finally asked the kids if they would like to go to that church and they said a resounding yes! I never will forget that first Sunday that we went. The kids wanted to go back that night. So we did. And then they wanted to go Wednesday night. After about a month of that, I let go of the tight grip I had on the pew, walked down the aisle at Northside Baptist Church, and all I said was, I need God in my life. In the last twenty-eight years I have had good times and bad times, but He was always there. I need Him just as much today as I did then. Don't wait another day. Call out to Him. He is there waiting for you. Just as you are."

How many of you are ready to release that death grip on your chains once and for all? Whether you're reading this as a believer or not, you might be in a place where you just feel ready to let go and let God. Even believers sometimes need to re-dedicate their hearts. Step back and take a look at your life and the legacy you are currently leaving. My mama wanted to be better. She felt called for more. She knew she needed God if she was going to make the most of the situation she was in. She put aside her feelings and put her family first. When she says, "Even worse, some of them knew me," she means they saw her for who she used to be. But y'all, God sees you for who you actually are. He knows you. *They* don't know you. He knows what you *can* be. You are so much more than your past mistakes. She was so much more than divorced and poor. She just needed to believe it. I thank God she did. I don't know what we would have done without the church family. Of course, there were plenty of things I didn't like about church as a kid. Getting up early, following rules, wearing dresses, and comparing myself to the members who were a little more well off than we were. But as an adult and mother looking back, I can see how much my mom needed those people. She needed an atmosphere where she could nurture a relationship with God and learn how to do better. She held our life to a higher standard (which I rebelled against plenty of times), but it was always about our character. We needed that part of our story for what God knew our future could hold.

God will often call you to step out of your comfort zone. It's there that He can show you how to take what you've been through to do something bigger than you. You will never be fearless of what doesn't come naturally to you. But the good news is that courage isn't the absence of fear; it's stepping forward *in spite of it*. This means you're capable of stretching beyond what's easy for you and being better for it.

There's never been a time when I've put together a funny video that a piece of me didn't feel afraid. There's never been a time when I spoke on a stage and my knees didn't shake. I've never created a single blog, vlog, video, or poem without wondering if I made a mistake. Stepping into your purpose will *always* make you nervous. It takes courage. And God takes over from there; you only need to trust Him. You'll make plenty of mistakes, but if He lets you fall on your face, remember He can't heal you for the better if you never break. So say goodbye to the fear chains.

I recently watched the movie *I Can Only Imagine*, which tells the story behind the hit Christian song by the lead singer of MercyMe, Bart Millard. His father had been an abusive drunk Bart's entire life. But then Bart witnessed him transform from a complete monster to a man passionately in love with Jesus. He saw how God changed his father into a man he loved and wanted to be like. Witnessing the melting of a heart of stone incites such inspiration. In Bart's case, it led to a song that blew billboards away and touched the hearts of millions.

The salvation of those struggling the most is the greatest reflection of the depth of God's love. The power He has to soften the hardest of hearts is made clear in the redemption of the fallen. Not the Jesus stickers on the back window of a car (although I do need to get me one of those off the Amazon). Not prayers left behind in the pews at church once a week. Not the rules of religion followed by people with no compassion. It's the *lost* He's after. Not the self-righteous found. We can't bring people to the Lord with our butts planted in the pews. We can't convince anyone that they are just as worthy as we are of God's mercy and grace while scoffing at their sinful ways.

John 3:16 is a well-known scripture, but the one *after* it needs to be heard. John 3:17 says, "For God did not send his Son into the world to *condemn* the world, but to save the world through him" (emphasis added). God did *not* send His Son to condemn, so who are we to pick and choose who is qualified for grace? When someone doesn't look like you, talk like you, or fit the image of a Christian, have you ever stopped to consider that they are exactly what God is looking for in a disciple? It's the fallen who get back up and inspire others to do the same. Guilt and condemnation do not come from the Lord, so check yourself before allowing the enemy to use you and your Christian background to crush someone's hope of joining the club. Our purpose in life as believers, however God works it through us, is to be a demonstration of the love shown to us. And sometimes that means swallowing our pride, calming our flesh, and loving those we don't even like.

———

"Love God" and "love others" are literally the two most important commandments we have been given. Jesus said, " 'Love the Lord your God with all your heart and with all your soul and with all your strength and with all your mind'; and, 'Love your neighbor as yourself' " (Luke 10:27). Jesus didn't say to love others *if they live like you.* To love others *if they look like you.* To love others *if they agree with you.* No! Just quite simply, love others. The world might not treat you with much love when you stand apart from it, but you're an oddball. . .remember?

I personally don't feel it's possible to love others if we haven't accepted that we are loved. If we haven't died to ourselves, we haven't really let go of our own troubles. Death to self means laying down our pride, letting go of control, admitting our faults, accepting forgiveness, bringing our demons to the surface, and dealing so we can heal. You can't die to your flesh and all of its baggage while hanging on to the ways of the world. It's *not* normal to accept and love those who hurt us, hurt others, or live life from a different set of values than we do. But you aren't normal anymore. You've died to your flesh, been made new, and now know how to live for others. You can't die to yourself and still be all about you. You learn how to love others by digging deep into the love Christ has for you. I know it doesn't make sense. And it certainly won't make sense to those around you. But the light of your spirit is *supposed* to set you apart. The enemy will put you through hell for it too. But like I've said before, what the devil doesn't realize is that when he puts you through hell, God will give you fuel from the fire. Sister, I'm telling you there is no devil in hell and no human on earth who can keep you from your purpose once you decide to follow Jesus. To yourself you have died, and there goes that chain of pride.

The old hymn says, "I have decided to follow Jesus."
I have *decided*. You know what? I know life has been
hard and I've suffered so much. But I've decided. I've
decided to put myself aside and live for Him. I've decided to put my emotions in time-out and help somebody else. I've decided to show kindness in the face
of hate. I've decided to show mercy when I long for
revenge. I've decided that nothing I want matters
because *His* will be done, not mine.

Living this way isn't easy. All I know is the decision
is made. When God puts a good word on my heart
and asks me to speak it, but I'm scared, I'll just have to
feel the fear and do it anyway. People ask me how I do
it. There is no how. I've *decided*. When God asks me
to forgive someone who doesn't deserve it and I don't
want to, I'll suck it up and do it anyhow. Ohhh, some
of y'all are like, *I can't though—you don't even understand*. Yes, I do; and yes, you can. You're not gonna be
bound anymore by the shackles of resentment. This is
a chain you *have* to shake if you want to change. You
have to understand that forgiving someone is not en-
dorsing wrong; it's not saying what someone did was
okay; it's not symbolizing a desire to have a relationship with someone. Forgiving someone is something
you do *for you*. Because you've been forgiven when
you didn't deserve it. In Luke 7:47, Jesus says he who

is forgiven little loves little. He forgave a woman of many sins because she loved much. Forgiveness is a reflection of love in your heart. If you won't forgive, your unforgiveness will sow a seed of anger within you. It will get in the way of your ability to love. You need to let go and let God have any wrongs that have been done to you. He will deal in due time with anyone who has sinned against you. Don't carry a burden that will make your soul sick. Let that chain go, and I bet your anger toward others won't be so quick.

Once you've decided to die to yourself, you forfeit what *you* want for what God wants from you, because you know that what He wants you to do is for your own good and, more importantly, for the good of others. You want to be used by Him? You want to fulfill your purpose in life? Start trusting what He tugs at you to do. Stop fighting Him on the small things, and you'll start receiving the bigger promises. Some of you haven't gotten that promotion because you refuse to do the laundry. LOL. Seriously, though. You want *more* responsibilities when you don't have authority over the dirty clothes yet? Some of you don't have the character for that raise, because God can't get you to stop shopping online. (QVC Easy Pay. Cough, cough.) Some of you can't get past your insecurity because you refuse to lift others up. Maybe you haven't conquered confidence because you won't quit with the gossip. Maybe you're asking God for something, but what you're doing results in the opposite outcome. Like wanting to be carefree, but wallowing in every horrible story on the news each morning. It's one thing to be aware of what's happening in the world, but another to seek out from sunup to sundown every detail of every tragedy, every death, every opinion, and every political scandal.

How are you supposed to walk around with the joy of the Lord when every day you soak in the evil of the world? I'm just saying, give more time and attention to things that lift you up than to things that drag you down. Worry will only steal away any chance of a good day. So train your brain to stay away from worries that leave you drained. Snap that chain. Know what you need to know and move your attention to what God wants *you* doing to make the world a better place. Don't get caught up in distractions that serve no purpose other than blurring your focus. Not today, Devil. (I just need you to know that anytime I say "Not today, Devil," I'm picturing the GIF of the preacher stomping across the stage behind the pulpit waving his Bible around. It makes me cackle.)

. . . And another thang. Don't confuse conviction with condemnation. Conviction is guidance. It's

God's way of correcting us so we can move forward, grow, learn, and be the best version of ourselves. One time I found twenty dollars on the floor at the Walmarts. I had a "What would you do?" moment where I imagined myself putting it in my purse and heading for the door only to be met with lights and cameras. John Quiñones and his "caught ya" smirk saying to me, "Now, you put the money in your purse. Did you think maybe it might belong to someone close by who really needed it, or were you just thinking of yourself?" I know it's so silly, but I just couldn't keep the money. I wasn't even living for the Lord at this time, but His conviction ain't reserved just for Christians. I was a broke college student. I *really* could have used that money. I wanted to think it was "the universe" taking care of me, but I couldn't get my stupid conscience to shut up and let me have it. I now know that voice wasn't me at all. But at the time, I was genuinely annoyed with myself. I walked up to customer service to turn it in, knowing there was no way for them to ever know whose it was. The customer service lady would probably just keep it. Her eyes got so wide when I handed over the money. She just looked at me like, *Errrkay?* I'll honestly never know why God wouldn't let me have that money. I'm betting it wound up in the hands of someone who had been praying for a blessing. Someone who needed it more than me. On that day I showed Him that even as a sleepy young Christian who had no relationship with Him, I had it in me to listen to my convictions.

God can't use anyone who won't hear Him. He needs a vessel willing to walk His way even when they don't want to. Even when it makes no sense. But when you do, off breaks the chain of condemnation. When you know the difference between condemnation and conviction, you'll be able to discern, learn, and listen. Condemnation keeps you right where you are, miserable and hopeless. It will have you slumped down with doubt, regret, and insecurity. Conviction teaches you what's better for your life. It provides guidance and light. Plus, it feels like love. When you're convicted of something, you don't feel bad about it. You just feel corrected and wiser. You know God is telling you something that is going to benefit you and make your life better. Condemnation makes you feel like backtracking, rebelling, or hiding under a rock. But...not today, Devil. (Okay, okay, I won't say it again until I say it again. It's just so funny.)

———

Life is hard, y'all. That's all there is to it. Life is full of never-ending ups and downs. Things are great sometimes, and things suck sometimes. But the *feeling* in my soul that can't be expressed in words is worth more than anything thrown at me from the world. *It is well with my soul.* I am ready to leave behind every lie I used to believe. I know it's hard for some to understand, but this is my story. I said to God, "If You give me a platform, I'll give You the glory." And just like that, everything changed. My heart, my soul, my thoughts, my words, my actions. I've learned that love hurts. The deeper you love someone, the harder it is to let them go. But it's my pain that has given me compassion. I'm learning to tell the difference between opportunity and distraction. I'm learning perfection doesn't exist, and we are blessed with our mess. I know without a doubt that I am worthy of His love and so are you. Even if you can't stand me, I can love you. Not all prayers are answered the way you want, but the conversation brings you closer. Being a Christian means to love God and love others. *Period.* What you say and how you say it matters.

Becoming the person God created you to be is a process. Enjoy the journey. One by one, let go of the chains you carry. They look a little different for each of us. Guilt, shame, worry, insecurity. They are all the things holding you back from believing you are loved, gifted, called, capable, and worthy. Self-reflect every day and journal your thoughts. Say your prayers and let the revelation come. Acknowledge your pain, and lay it down so you can heal. Don't let anyone tell you what you can and cannot do with your life.

> Despite what the world says, you can turn your
>   chains into reins.
> Know who you are and be seen,
> Let your rock bottom be your awakening.
> Take purpose from your pain,
> Stop hiding away.
> Let your flesh die and let God do His thing.
> Let your ripples be loving; your suffering isn't
>   for nothing.
> Embrace your mistakes.
> Once and for all,
> Break the freaking chains!

I promise you this: everything you've been through that has made you feel unworthy and unloved is what actually makes you odd(ly) enough!

About the Author

Carolanne Miljavac is a southern-raised, Jesus-saved, barely sane author, speaker, social media goofball, wife, and mom of three daughters. It was the crushing loss of her seven-year-old niece to cancer that finally humbled her enough to listen to God when He said to her, as she crumbled in her car, *"Give it up."* Without the chains of fear and insecurity, she followed her spirit's instruction to speak. She now has over 100 million video views and nearly half a million social media followers. A true reflection of "beauty for ashes," Carolanne has become the go-to girl for a good laugh, motivation, loving truths, and vulnerability. She pulls heartstrings while tapping funny bones with a message of freedom and revelation. Her purpose in life is to spread love and joy without sacrificing honesty and truth. She believes we all have a story needing to be told. Grief taught her gratitude, pain gave her purpose, and loss revealed true love. With faith, she found audacity, and her mission is to give you the guts to be *you* too.